KRISTEN PARKER

The Spells We Wove with Forgotten Words

Copyright © 2025 by Kristen Parker

All rights reserved. No part of this publication may be reproduced, stored or transmitted in any form or by any means, electronic, mechanical, photocopying, recording, scanning, or otherwise without written permission from the publisher. It is illegal to copy this book, post it to a website, or distribute it by any other means without permission.

This novel is entirely a work of fiction. The names, characters and incidents portrayed in it are the work of the author's imagination. Any resemblance to actual persons, living or dead, events or localities is entirely coincidental.

Kristen Parker asserts the moral right to be identified as the author of this work.

Kristen Parker has no responsibility for the persistence or accuracy of URLs for external or third-party Internet Websites referred to in this publication and does not guarantee that any content on such Websites is, or will remain, accurate or appropriate.

Designations used by companies to distinguish their products are often claimed as trademarks. All brand names and product names used in this book and on its cover are trade names, service marks, trademarks and registered trademarks of their respective owners. The publishers and the book are not associated with any product or vendor mentioned in this book. None of the companies referenced within the book have endorsed the book.

First edition

This book was professionally typeset on Reedsy.
Find out more at reedsy.com

Contents

1	The Shimmer in the Library	1
2	The Man in the Mirror	9
3	The Forgotten Words	21
4	Tangled Threads	31
5	The Spell That Unmakes	41
6	Whispers of the First Time	54
7	The Pact of Ash and Flame	65
8	A Memory Shared	75
9	The Curse Unfolds	85
10	Love in a Loop	95
11	The Betrayer's Mark	106
12	The Hollow Moon Rises	116
13	The Archive of Echoes	126
14	Fire Between Us	137
15	The Truth of Us	149
16	When Love Was Magic	159
17	The Final Weaving	169
18	Blood for Memory	178
19	The Spell Unraveled	187
20	The Name in the Wind	199

One

The Shimmer in the Library

The wind clawed at the crumbling façade of the fallen Academy of Magic, its song a symphony of forgotten things. Aetherwyn, once the jewel of arcane study, now lay in spectral silence. The great city still stood—its spires twisting toward the heavens like the fingers of the gods—but beneath its elegant veneer were places time refused to remember. And Kaela Dorne had learned long ago that those were the places worth finding.

A lantern swung from her hand, golden light catching in the dust that danced through the darkness. Her boots echoed off the cold marble as she descended the staircase into what had once been the Grand Library. Age had gnawed at the arches. Shelves stood like grave markers, books long burned or buried. Her breath plumed before her in the chill air.

Kaela brushed a strand of black hair from her cheek, tucking it behind her ear. Her other hand clutched the handle of a canvas satchel weighed down by scrolls, chalk, and a dagger with an obsidian hilt. One never knew what crawled in the deep places anymore.

"Third shelf from the left," she whispered to herself, fingers trailing along a cracked pillar inscribed with sigils faded nearly to nothing. "Section on temporal anomalies. Theory of recursive arcana. Language fragments... yes."

The records had pointed her here. Not official records—those had been scrubbed long ago—but the whisperings of another mad scholar who had scrawled theories across temple walls and grave markers. He'd believed something dangerous had once been stored deep in the Academy. A spell not meant to be cast. A name no one dared to speak.

She moved deeper, heart thrumming in her chest. The silence was absolute.

A flicker of movement—light where there was none.

She froze.

The shimmer danced like oil on water, hovering in the air near a collapsed reading dais. No source. No spell circle. Just magic... waiting.

Kaela narrowed her eyes. "Residual spelllock?" she murmured.

Cautiously, she approached. The shimmer pulsed. Something tugged at her gut, a pull she couldn't name. Like longing. Like sorrow.

She reached into her satchel, fingers brushing past chalk, until she found a small piece of silver glass etched with runes. Holding it up, she whispered, "Revela."

The shimmer cracked like ice fracturing on a lake. With a hum, the air split open—and a section of the floor fell away, revealing a staircase that descended beneath the bones of the library.

"Oh gods," she breathed. "It's real."

The Vault of Silenced Spells.

She descended, the air growing colder with each step. The walls were lined in obsidian, etched with warnings in a dozen dead tongues. She translated them silently.

He who binds love to time shall lose both.
Memory is the first cost. Name is the last.
Do not speak the words once forgotten.

She reached the bottom.

A single pedestal stood at the heart of the chamber. Upon it, an open tome. Dustless. Waiting.

Kaela stepped forward.

The text shimmered, inked in gold that refused to stay still. The letters shifted, curled, reformed.

But she understood them.

Every word felt like a blade drawn across her soul.

The spell was incomplete. Fractured. But powerful—beyond anything she'd read.

A memory-binding incantation.

Forbidden.

Not just forgotten—**erased.**

As her eyes moved over the final line, her breath caught. A name was carved into the corner of the page, small and precise. Not part of the spell.

Just a name.

Ezren.

She staggered back.

The name rang through her skull like a bell. It meant nothing—yet everything. Her knees hit the stone.

She whispered it again. "Ezren."

The room trembled.

From the shadows, a figure stirred.

Kaela rose, hand reaching for her dagger—but the figure was gone. Only the shimmer of magic remained.

She snapped the book shut. The chamber groaned as if in pain.

Time twisted around her.

Something had awoken.

And she had spoken the first forgotten word.

Kaela's breath steamed in the frozen air, her fingers trembling as she pressed them to the worn cover of the book. The chill no longer came from the stones or the ancient vault—it pulsed from within her, as if the spell had dug into her bones, clawing up through her chest to wrap around her throat.

"Ezren…" she said again, voice hoarse, reverent. The name vibrated through her like a tuning fork struck at the soul. It didn't feel like discovery.

It felt like remembering.

A sound. Soft. Scraping.

She froze.

Beyond the shimmer, something moved again—not a shimmer this time, but shadow. The shape of a man, just beyond the curve of the chamber's columns. He stood still. Watching.

"Who's there?" she asked sharply, stepping back with one hand on the dagger at her belt. Her voice bounced back to her from the chamber walls, distorted. Too many echoes. Too many answers.

The shadow didn't answer. It didn't advance. But it didn't vanish either.

Kaela summoned light. Her fingers traced a quick sigil in

the air, whispering the incantation under her breath. A pulse of flame burst in her palm—and the shadow vanished, leaving only stillness in its wake.

Not a man. Not a beast. Not a memory. Something else.

She turned back to the pedestal.

The tome was no longer open.

But she hadn't shut it.

It had closed itself.

The hum of magic rose. Not angry—but ancient. Alive.

Kaela's pulse quickened. She didn't believe in fate. She didn't believe in destiny or signs or whispered omens.

But in that moment, staring at the sealed book, she felt the unbearable weight of something long dormant—watching her. Choosing her.

She slid the tome into her satchel, the weight of it pulling against her shoulder like iron shackles. She began the ascent, boots striking the obsidian stairs, heart pounding in rhythm with the silent spells pressed into the walls.

He who binds love to time shall lose both.

The words echoed again, louder this time.

At the threshold of the shattered floor, the shimmer flared. Kaela paused. She reached out—fingertips grazing the rippling edge of magic—and stepped through.

Light flared, heat blossoming across her skin, then—

Silence.

The Grand Library was as she had left it. Still and cold. But… not quite.

Every candle on the long-dead chandeliers now flickered with pale flame.

Every broken window was whole again, casting moonlight across pristine floors.

And standing in the center of the aisle, where no one had been before, was a figure.

Male.

Tall, with a lean, shadowed frame wrapped in a black coat threaded with silver. His silver-blond hair shimmered in the candlelight, falling loose around sharp cheekbones and a mouth that looked carved from ice. His eyes—Kaela stopped breathing—glowed faintly, like dying stars.

He looked at her.

She stepped back, hand on her dagger.

The figure mirrored her.

Step for step.

She blinked. He vanished.

Not disappeared—gone, like a ghost flitting behind the veil.

Kaela swore, her voice echoing again. Too many echoes.

She wasn't alone. Not anymore.

And worse—something had shifted. The entire library thrummed with magic. Not the dead, dormant kind that clung to ruins. This was **present**. **Alive**. Like it had been waiting for someone to break the seal.

She moved quickly through the hall, ascending the ruined central staircase into the city above. As she passed beneath the last arch, a gust of wind tore through the corridor, slamming her satchel hard against her side.

The tome pulsed.

Like a heartbeat.

She pressed a hand to it, her breath catching.

Then she heard it—just barely, on the edge of the wind. A whisper, too soft to be speech.

A word with no sound.

But she **knew** what it was.

The Shimmer in the Library

Ezren.

—

Above ground, the air had turned sharp and cold. Aetherwyn's towers loomed around her, moonlight casting the whole city in blue-silver light. Kaela paused at the edge of the broken library steps, eyes scanning the empty plaza.

A boy walked past, head down, cloak drawn tight against the wind. He didn't look up, didn't speak—but as he passed, Kaela's skin prickled.

His shadow didn't match his step.

She turned to follow, but the boy had vanished between two alleyways.

This city is haunted, she thought grimly. Not by ghosts. By memory.

Her footsteps took her to the edge of the Scholar's Quarters, where the oldest buildings had been half-swallowed by vines and ivy. Her room—her sanctuary—was just above a disused apothecary. She pushed the door open with a creak and slipped inside.

The scent of parchment and lavender filled her lungs. She bolted the door, drew the curtains, and only then did she let her satchel drop to the floor.

The tome thudded.

She didn't dare open it again. Not yet.

Instead, Kaela moved to the mirror above the basin. Her reflection stared back at her—wide violet-gray eyes, pale skin, hair wind-tangled and wild. But behind her own eyes, something had changed.

She was no longer alone in her own memory.

She leaned in closer.

The mirror darkened. For the briefest moment—barely a

breath—another face looked back at her.

A man's face.

His lips moved.

Her heart skipped.

Then, nothing. Only her own stunned reflection.

Kaela stumbled back, heart in her throat.

She didn't scream.

She simply whispered, like a prayer, like a curse, "Ezren…"

And the candlelight in the room flared.

—

Far across the city, in a crumbling watchtower long abandoned, another figure stirred.

He stood in darkness, firelight crackling low beside him. His coat hung from his shoulders, one hand curled tight around a crystal pendant glowing faintly red. His other hand pressed to his temple, jaw clenched.

He saw her.

Just for a moment.

A flicker. A flash.

Violet-gray eyes. A voice he didn't remember—but one he missed like breath.

He didn't know her name.

Didn't know his own.

But something inside him whispered, **soon**.

The magic was waking.

And so was he.

Two

The Man in the Mirror

The sea below roared like a wounded beast, crashing its fury against the jagged cliffs of Carrowind. Wind howled through the bones of the old tower, where the stones were blackened with age and magic, and the floor still bore the burns of spells cast in desperation. Ezren Valen stood in the heart of it, coat whipping at his calves, his breath misting in the cold. The glass shard in his hand trembled with more than just the wind.

It was happening again.

She was there—her eyes violet-gray, her mouth forming his name with aching softness—but only for a moment. Just long enough for the recognition to ignite and vanish like fire through frost.

Then the reflection turned to his own face—wild, gaunt, hollow-eyed.

He hurled the shard across the room.

It struck the wall and exploded into silver splinters.

Ezren's hands braced against the edge of the wooden table, the runes carved into its surface glowing faintly in response to his rage. Power rippled from his skin in tight pulses, untethered, unshaped. The tower groaned.

He forced himself to breathe.

Again.

And again.

It wasn't the first time he'd seen her.

The woman—always in mirrors, pools, the sheen of polished metal—appeared without warning. Never spoke. Never stayed. But each time, her gaze carved a little deeper into him.

And the name…

Ezren.

She said it like it belonged to her.

He didn't know who she was. He barely knew who *he* was. Only that the name he wore had once meant something else. That magic clung to him like smoke to flame. That he had lived before and forgotten it. Not by choice.

By design.

He pushed away from the table, stalked toward the spiral stairwell, and descended into the lower level of the tower. Crates and tomes lined the walls, all filled with things he'd collected over the years—objects that stirred recognition in him though he couldn't remember why.

At the center of the room, a basin sat atop a pedestal. The water shimmered like moonlight, even though the tower had no windows on this level. It wasn't just a scrying pool.

It was a fracture in time.

And tonight, the shimmer had returned.

Ezren's hand hovered over it. His fingers twitched, as if

something on the other side called to him.

He didn't need a spell to see her. Not anymore.

She came without summons. As if some thread between them had been stretched taut—straining toward reunion.

The water rippled.

Her face bloomed into view. Pale, fierce. Hair unbound by any braid or comb. Her lips parted as if she were about to speak. But the sound never reached him.

He leaned closer.

This time, her hand lifted, mirroring his.

His fingers grazed the water.

And the basin shattered.

A shockwave knocked him off his feet. Light flared, hot and searing, and for an instant Ezren saw—no, *felt*—something that wasn't his. Stone walls lined with obsidian. A golden tome. The sound of his name gasped like a prayer. Her voice.

Kaela.

His back struck the floor, breath ripped from his lungs.

The magic pulsed again, sharp as a blade behind his eyes. When the pain passed, he lay there staring up at the cracked ceiling, heart pounding like a war drum.

Kaela.

He knew it now.

The name rang through him like an oath sealed in blood and fire.

He crawled to the basin—now shattered, water steaming on the stone floor—and reached for a small sliver of the crystal rim. When his fingers closed around it, the vision surged forward again.

But it wasn't just her face this time.

It was **words**.

Not spoken. Not read. *Felt*.

A spell. In a tongue that shouldn't exist anymore.

One he'd once spoken.

One that had erased everything.

He staggered to his feet, legs unsteady. The memories hadn't returned—but a path had. A direction. A thread to follow.

And he would.

He had no choice.

Ezren rode through the veil of midnight fog on the back of a charcoal-black steed, cloaked in silence. The path toward Aetherwyn wound like a scar through the mountains, slick with mist and memory. He didn't remember the city, not fully—but it clawed at something beneath his ribs. A place that had known him. Hated him. Loved him.

He passed silent watchtowers and forgotten shrines, all abandoned since the collapse of the magical academies. Magic was feared now. Hunted.

Especially the kind that Ezren carried in his blood.

The kind that broke time.

Hours passed. Dawn approached like a secret, and as he neared the edge of the city, he dismounted beside a jagged wall of broken statues. All bore the sigils of ancient houses now dissolved or disgraced. His boots crunched over shattered stone and bone-white petals from some stubborn bloom that still grew in the ruins.

He followed the pull.

The residue of a spell so potent it still whispered on the wind.

He reached a square of cracked cobblestone and froze.

At the center, half-swallowed by time and ivy, stood the ruins of the Academy Library.

He remembered now.

Not clearly. Not yet.

But enough.

He pushed open the scorched door and stepped inside.

Ash. Dust. Silence.

And magic.

It hummed under his skin like a storm waiting to break.

He moved through the shadows of broken shelves, past the skeletons of forgotten knowledge, until he found a scorch mark on the marble floor. Still warm.

Someone had been here.

Recently.

And had opened something that should have remained sealed.

Ezren knelt, fingers brushing the floor. He closed his eyes and murmured a phrase. The residue answered, curling up his arm like smoke. Gold, threaded with violet. Her magic.

Kaela.

Still fresh.

Still close.

He tracked her across the city, following fragments of her power like breadcrumbs scattered through the ether. They led him not to palaces or towers, but to a modest room above an apothecary. From the alley below, he watched the candlelight flicker against the curtain.

Then the shadow of her.

She stood before the mirror, hand pressed to the glass.

His breath caught.

Even across the distance, he could feel it.

Their bond.

Not new. Not recent.

Old. Deep. Frayed, but unbroken.

He moved toward the back door.

Stopped.

He couldn't just walk in. Not now. Not when he didn't even know what he'd done to her. What he'd taken.

Instead, he reached for the polished silver coin in his pocket. A relic from a lifetime he couldn't name. He whispered a word into it, lacing the magic with memory and desire, then flipped it into the open air toward her window.

It would find its way to her.

It always had.

Then he turned and vanished into the night.

In a room warmed by candlelight and still haunted by visions, Kaela sat before the mirror. The silver shimmer had gone still.

But her heart hadn't.

She touched her reflection, as if to trace something she couldn't see—but felt.

Then something struck the window.

She turned.

There, on the sill, lay a silver coin.

She approached it slowly.

Lifted it.

It was warm.

On the back, a symbol—two interlocking runes. One she knew. One she didn't.

A strange emotion welled in her chest. Longing. Fear. Recognition.

And something else.

Hope.

Her fingers closed around the coin as the wind rose.

In the glass behind her, a man's voice whispered her name.

And for the first time, she didn't flinch.

The Man in the Mirror

She smiled.

The next morning arrived in fragments—sunlight breaking through the clouds like slivers of prophecy, the city of Aetherwyn wrapped in a haze that blurred the line between waking and dreaming. From the rooftop of a half-crumbled bell tower, Ezren sat with his back to the rising sun, the taste of old spells and rusted guilt still thick on his tongue.

He had not slept.

Not really.

Every time he closed his eyes, the dreams came.

Kaela's voice. The brush of her hand. The scream of a world breaking apart.

And then... silence.

He ran a gloved hand through his hair and stared at the skyline. The towers and spires of Aetherwyn shimmered in the morning haze like ghosts, and beyond them—beneath them—the veins of the old city pulsed with hidden magic. He could feel it more clearly now. The spell was waking.

He had cast it.

He was almost certain of that.

And yet... he had no memory of doing so. Only the scars it left in its wake. Holes in his mind where years should have been. Names missing. Faces blurred.

But Kaela... her name had survived.

Even when all else had been burned away.

He pulled a small, cracked book from his coat and flipped it open to the middle. The pages were empty, save for a single phrase scratched into the paper in desperate, slanted script:

Find her before the eclipse. Or forget forever.

Ezren didn't remember writing it.

But he believed it.

And the clock was already ticking.

He rose, cloak snapping in the wind, and descended the tower steps two at a time. The magic still clung to the air from Kaela's visit to the Vault. Her aura left impressions—shimmers in space that only a trained eye could follow.

Or someone like him.

Someone cursed by the spell he'd once cast.

In a dim corner of the city's lower district, Ezren passed beneath the arch of an ancient aqueduct. A stream of black feathers scattered into the air from a broken barrel—crows startled from a hidden perch. His boots struck the stone rhythmically, his shadow trailing behind him like a second soul.

He was being followed.

He could feel it. A flutter against the edge of his awareness, like eyes pressed into the back of his skull. But every time he turned—nothing.

No movement. No magic. No presence.

Still, he kept one hand close to the runes carved into his bracer.

Whoever they were, they were good.

But not as good as him.

Not yet.

He ducked into a side corridor, pressed himself into shadow, and waited.

Ten breaths. Twenty.

Then the figure moved.

A ripple—barely perceptible—across the reflection of a puddle.

Ezren struck.

The Man in the Mirror

He twisted out of the alley, flung his hand forward, and muttered a sharp incantation. Light erupted, searing through the air like lightning in reverse. The figure hissed and flung up a ward just in time.

The blast struck and shattered it.

They tumbled backward into the alley.

Ezren stalked forward, boot on the stranger's chest.

"Who are you?" he growled. "Who sent you?"

The figure coughed, hood falling back.

A girl—barely twenty, with sun-darkened skin and sharp amber eyes.

"I'm not your enemy," she wheezed.

"Not convincing," Ezren said, pressing harder.

She shoved a small pendant into the air between them.

The symbol made his stomach twist.

Two spirals, intertwined—one gold, one red.

The mark of the **Order of the Silenced**.

Ezren's hand moved before he thought. The sigil burst into flame in her hand, and she screamed, rolling away from him, clutching her palm.

"I'm not one of them!" she shouted. "Not anymore!"

He stilled, wariness crawling up his spine. "Then why wear their mark?"

"To get close. To *warn* her. Kaela Dorne is in danger."

He froze.

The girl pushed herself to her knees, breathing hard.

"They know she found the Vault. They felt the spell awaken. The Order will come for her."

Ezren stared at her, disbelief warring with dread.

"You're lying."

She met his eyes. "Would you really take that chance?"

The Spells We Wove with Forgotten Words

Silence. Heavy. Weighted.

He pulled her to her feet with a rough tug. "If you're lying to me—"

"I'm not."

"Then we leave now."

"For where?"

"To find her."

Kaela sat at her writing desk, staring at the silver coin that hadn't stopped glowing since dawn. It pulsed every few minutes, as though timed to a heartbeat.

Not hers.

His.

She hadn't slept either.

The dreams were growing worse. No longer shadows and whispers—but memories she couldn't remember having. A sword in her hand. A city burning. Ezren, reaching for her, blood on his hands. A kiss that tasted like goodbye.

She closed her fist around the coin and stood.

It was time to stop waiting.

She packed a satchel with notes, the tome from the Vault, a small vial of phoenix ash, and a blade carved from bone-iron. Then she wrapped her coat tight and made her way down to the street.

Aetherwyn pulsed around her. Too loud. Too bright.

The wind whispered her name.

And somewhere in the crowd, she felt *him*.

Ezren.

Just as she turned the corner, a man stepped into her path.

He was tall, cloaked in black, with silver-blond hair and eyes like breaking storms.

She knew him instantly.

Not from memory.

But from feeling.

"Ezren," she whispered.

He exhaled her name like it was the first breath after drowning.

And the world tilted.

For a single, breathless second, everything stood still.

Then the magic exploded.

From the rooftops, arrows of shadow screamed through the air.

The Order had found them.

Ezren threw up a ward just as the first bolt hit. The girl from before—his unexpected ally—shouted a warning and drew twin knives from her belt.

Kaela dove, rolling behind a stone column, hand flying to the runes on her palm. The spell activated in an instant—light bursting from her fingers in a dome of golden fire.

Ezren's voice found her through the chaos.

"Run! The spell's not complete—we're still vulnerable!"

Kaela shouted back, "Then finish it!"

"I can't. Not alone."

The air cracked.

A dozen robed figures descended from the roofs, hoods fluttering like dying wings, eyes glowing with white fire.

Ezren grabbed Kaela's hand.

And in that moment—their magic fused.

Gold and stormlight. Memory and fire.

It wasn't enough to stop the Order.

But it was enough to buy them time.

He muttered a single word.

The world bent.

And they vanished.

Only the burning symbol of two intertwined spirals remained behind—scorched into the stone.

A warning.

A reckoning.

And a promise.

Three

The Forgotten Words

The storm had rolled in fast—too fast.

One moment, Aetherwyn basked in pale morning light; the next, the sky was a canvas of darkened slate, thunder grumbling in its chest like an omen. Rain battered the cobbled streets with sudden fury, chasing vendors beneath awnings and sending horses into skittish fits. The wind swept through the avenues, tugging at cloaks and signs, moaning like some spirit lost between time.

Kaela pulled her hood tighter, eyes downcast, her boots splashing through puddles as she wove through the alleys of the Scholar's District. Her thoughts tangled with the lingering presence of Ezren—his name echoed still in the hollow of her chest, and every reflective surface teased his shadow. The coin he'd sent her still hummed with heat beneath the fold of her cloak, but it offered no direction, no guidance—just *presence*.

She clutched the satchel close to her hip. Inside, the

forbidden tome pulsed softly, the letters shifting when she dared glance at them, curling into languages dead for centuries. Words that didn't stay put. Words that breathed.

Kaela's fingers itched to read them again. But something in her gut warned against it. Not here. Not yet.

A crack rang out behind her—sharp, clean.

She froze.

The street was empty, but her senses prickled. Rain fell steady, but no footsteps followed hers. No carriages moved. No merchants called. The silence pressed in around her like a hand closing over her mouth.

She turned a corner and stopped.

Three figures stood ahead.

Hooded. Robed in deep gray, trimmed in silver thread. Their faces were shadowed by bone-white masks, expressionless save for a single rune etched between the brows: **Silence**.

The Order.

Kaela stepped back, heart pounding, hand slipping toward her belt.

A fourth figure emerged behind her, quiet as breath.

She twisted, drawing the bone-iron dagger—but the figure caught her wrist mid-motion, squeezing until her fingers went numb.

"Kaela Dorne," came a voice like stone on steel. "Daughter of the Forgotten Line."

She yanked free and staggered back, eyes wide. "How do you know my name?"

The figure tilted its head. "You are the echo of your mother. You bear the blood of the memory-weavers. That is a crime we cannot allow to persist."

"I'm just a scholar," she said quickly, mind racing. "You've

The Forgotten Words

got the wrong person—"

"You opened the Vault," another intoned. "You spoke the name."

Kaela's mouth went dry.

The spell. The tome. Ezren.

She took a step back. Then another. "I didn't mean to—"

"Meaning is irrelevant. Words spoken, once heard, cannot be unheard."

The first figure drew a blade—long, silver-black, flickering with wardlight. Rain hissed off its edge like steam.

Kaela turned to run.

A wall of air struck her, flinging her into the cobblestones.

Pain splintered through her ribs. She coughed, tasted copper.

One of the masked figures advanced, hand outstretched. Lines of runes flared down his sleeve, channeling the spell—an unraveling spell, designed to pull memory apart thread by thread.

"Your mind is not yours," the figure whispered. "It must be cleaned."

Kaela screamed as the spell struck.

It felt like knives behind her eyes, unspooling thought, shattering sense. Faces blurred. Words bled. She clutched at her head, desperate to hold herself together.

Ezren.

That one thought screamed louder than the spell.

The moment his name formed in her mind, her hand moved without command.

She slammed her palm to the cobblestone.

A flash of light burst outward in a radius—bright, golden, burning.

The Order reeled back, arms raised, their magic unraveling

mid-cast.

Kaela didn't stop to question.

Her mouth moved of its own accord.

"Taran'el mor vethira—"

The words curled out of her in a tongue she had never studied, never read—yet it poured from her like breath.

A second pulse of light cracked through the street, rippling outward like a tidal wave of sound and time. The rain froze mid-fall. For one impossible moment, everything stopped.

And then the world *bent*.

The spell collapsed in on itself, sucking air and sound into a point no larger than a pinhead—and then it **exploded**.

The blast flung Kaela backward into a wall, the impact stealing the breath from her lungs. She crumpled to the ground as the storm howled louder, real thunder now rumbling in the heavens above.

When she opened her eyes, the Order was gone.

No bodies. No blood. Just an empty street and the smell of scorched stone.

Her chest heaved. Her hands trembled. The runes on her skin still glowed faintly.

"What the hell was that?" she whispered.

The rain began to fall again, heavier now, washing the scorched sigils from the ground.

Kaela stood slowly, bones protesting, and checked her satchel. The tome was still intact, though warm. Too warm.

The words had used her.

No—not just used. **Chosen.**

She staggered back toward her rooms, weaving through the alleys like a ghost. She couldn't go to the Academy. Not anymore. She couldn't trust the city guards, nor the magisters.

The Forgotten Words

The Order had infiltrated both.

And someone had told them about her.

That thought chilled her more than the rain.

Back in her sanctuary, she bolted the door and collapsed into a chair. Her hands ran through her hair, dragging wet strands away from her face.

The spell.

She had spoken it.

Words not spoken in centuries—maybe longer.

And they had *responded*.

Not just to her magic.

To **her blood**.

She reached for the tome and flipped it open.

The pages were no longer shifting.

They had stilled.

The spell had recognized her.

And written itself *in her hand*.

A phrase appeared on the page before her eyes, fresh ink forming as if written by an invisible quill:

"The one who speaks the forgotten words must choose— remember, or be remembered."

Kaela's blood ran cold.

She closed the tome.

But the words had already branded themselves across her soul.

And something inside her had awoken that would not sleep again.

The candlelight trembled.

Not from wind—there was none. Every window was latched shut, every door sealed with warding runes Kaela had etched herself in the margins of every frame. But the flame still flickered, sputtered, as if reacting to a pulse of unseen energy.

Kaela stared at the page.

"The one who speaks the forgotten words must choose—remember, or be remembered."

The ink had finished drying, but the letters seemed to hum—like they were alive, breathing on the page. Not ordinary magic. Something older. Wilder. And the worst part was, the choice the words offered... she didn't understand it.

Remember what?

Be remembered by whom?

She touched the edge of the parchment with trembling fingers. Her skin still hummed with the residual heat of the spell. The language she'd spoken was not recorded in any known lexicon. Not even the ancient runes from the Eastern War contained those syllables.

And yet, her voice had shaped them.

Spoken them.

From instinct.

As if they had waited in her blood, sleeping.

Kaela stood, pacing the narrow chamber, her damp cloak shedding water onto the worn rug. Lightning flashed through the curtains, outlining her silhouette like a ghost walking behind her own shadow.

The Order of the Silenced had come for her—and nearly won.

She hadn't been prepared. She hadn't even understood what she was carrying until the spell surged through her like fire.

And still... something in her *had* known. Deep in her marrow.

It wasn't just instinct.

The Forgotten Words

It was *remembrance*.

She spun back to the desk and tore open her satchel. Scrolls and notes scattered across the wood. Beneath them all was the coin Ezren had sent her—silver, faintly glowing, cool now to the touch but pulsing, like it still carried his essence.

She clutched it tightly.

"Ezren," she whispered.

The candle guttered again.

She didn't expect an answer.

But one came.

Not in words.

In a *vision*.

Not from her eyes, but from within.

A hand in hers—rough, calloused, gripping like he was trying to keep her from falling. Blood on their palms, mingling. A battlefield behind them, sky burning red. His voice: "Say the words, Kaela. Say them and I'll follow you through time itself."

She gasped, stumbling back from the desk, clutching her chest. The vision vanished.

The silence was oppressive, ringing in her ears louder than any scream.

That was not a dream.

It was a *memory*.

And it wasn't from this life.

Kaela blinked rapidly. She wasn't ready to believe it—yet her magic responded to it, resonated with it.

She had lived before.

She had known him before.

She had *loved* him before.

She looked at her palms. They were clean now, no blood, no bruises. But they trembled. She wasn't afraid of the spell she had cast.

She was afraid of what it meant.

A knock came at the door.

Kaela froze.

It was soft. Deliberate.

Not a neighbor. Not a merchant. And not the Order—they would never knock.

Her dagger was in her hand before she realized she'd drawn it.

"Who's there?" she called, voice steady despite the racing of her heart.

A pause.

Then—

"I'm not here to hurt you."

A man's voice.

Rough, like gravel softened by wind. Familiar in a way that made her bones ache.

She crossed the room, careful not to trip over scattered scrolls. Her hand hovered over the bolt.

She drew breath.

And opened the door.

Ezren stood there, rain misting the shoulders of his black coat, silver-blond hair damp, eyes shadowed and storm-bright. His presence hit her like a chord strummed in her chest—one she hadn't realized was stretched so tightly.

He looked at her like he *knew* her.

Like he'd been waiting for this moment longer than time itself.

"Kaela," he breathed.

She didn't speak.

Didn't move.

Couldn't.

Lightning cracked behind him, illuminating his features—and hers in the reflection of his eyes.

"You found the Vault," he said softly.

She nodded.

"You spoke the spell."

Another nod.

His expression changed—barely. A flicker of pain. Guilt.

She stepped back and let him in.

The air in the room shifted the moment he crossed the threshold. Magic trembled like a harp string plucked by an unseen hand.

They stood in silence.

The space between them charged, like the eye of a storm held still only by will.

Ezren looked at the tome, then at the scattered notes.

"I didn't mean for you to find it," he said.

Kaela's voice was low. "You sent me the coin."

"I didn't mean for you to find it *yet*."

She turned toward him, eyes sharp. "Why? Because the Order nearly unmade me in the street today?"

His jaw clenched. "Because the spell wasn't supposed to wake until we were ready. It's dangerous. It draws them to us."

"Well," she said, stepping forward, "it's awake. And so am I."

Ezren looked at her. Truly looked at her.

"You remembered something, didn't you?"

She didn't answer.

He stepped closer.

"Tell me what you saw."

Kaela hesitated.

Then whispered, "Blood. Our hands. A promise."

Ezren's breath caught.

"We said the spell before," he murmured. "A long time ago."

"You mean in another life?"

He nodded once.

She stared at him, at the haunted eyes and the weight he wore like armor.

"What are we?" she asked.

He reached out, touched her fingers—lightly, cautiously, reverently.

"Cursed," he said. "By our own love. By the magic we dared to cast."

A silence fell between them.

Outside, the rain softened to mist.

Inside, time stilled.

And Kaela whispered, "Then let's remember it together."

And the room lit with gold.

Four

Tangled Threads

The first thing Kaela noticed was the silence.

Not the kind born from absence or stillness, but something deeper—an oppressive hush that swallowed sound before it could form. Even her breath seemed muffled, as though the very air resisted her existence.

The world around her had changed.

One blink ago, she had been standing in her room in Aetherwyn, her fingers still warm from touching Ezren's hand, her heart still thunderous from his words. Then light—gold, blinding, burning—had wrapped around her like flame, and the floor had vanished beneath her feet.

Now she stood on a path of silver mist, suspended over an abyss with no bottom. Above, the sky stretched in hues that defied language—part night, part sunrise, and woven through with streaks of violet flame. The air shimmered as if the space between worlds had cracked, letting the truth bleed through.

The Veil Between.

She had read of it—once, in a forbidden footnote penned by a half-mad historian: *"Where time fractures and memory breathes, the lovers lost may walk again."*

Kaela took a step forward.

The path rippled beneath her feet.

Every instinct screamed that this place was not meant for mortals. The Veil wasn't a world. It was a wound. And yet something—some unseen tether—pulled her forward.

She passed under a broken archway made of fractured stone and whispered script. Words drifted through the air like falling leaves—names, languages, thoughts. Some she recognized. Others chilled her to the core.

Kaelarn, protector of the sealed gate...

Ezren, breaker of oaths...

Do not speak what was never meant to be heard...

She remembers the fire. He remembers the kiss...

Kaela paused, breath catching.

Ezren.

He was here.

Somehow, she knew it.

She quickened her pace, the mist winding tighter around her ankles as the path narrowed. Memories flickered at the corners of her vision—hers, but not. Past lives? Dreams? Echoes?

She saw herself dressed in armor, blade drawn, fire roaring behind her.

Ezren—laughing beside her on a grassy hill, holding a plum between his teeth.

Ezren—bleeding in her arms.

Ezren—pulling away.

"No," she whispered. "Not again."

Her footsteps slowed as she came to a clearing—a space where the path widened into a floating platform made of shattered stone, surrounded by mirrors that hung suspended in the air. Each one reflected something different—an image, a moment, a lifetime.

Kaela stepped toward one and gasped.

It showed her—standing atop a ruined tower in the rain, her arms wrapped around Ezren as magic surged through the air. His face buried in her hair, her mouth against his temple.

Another mirror reflected something else: her pushing him away, tears streaking her face, the tome in her hands glowing with unreadable runes.

Another—Kaela and Ezren as children, laughing beside a riverbank, chasing dragonflies with wooden swords.

She turned from them all, chest tightening.

None of it made sense. All of it felt *real*.

A sound behind her—a step.

She spun.

And there he was.

Ezren stood at the edge of the clearing, his coat stirring with the breeze, hair tousled by unseen wind. His eyes locked on hers, stunned. Caught. Like a man watching the stars fall.

They didn't speak.

They didn't need to.

Kaela stepped forward.

Ezren mirrored her.

One step.

Two.

They stopped a breath apart.

He reached out, his fingers grazing hers. The contact was electric—light flared between their skin, gold and violet dancing in sparks. It was more than touch. It was memory. Connection.

"Do I know you?" he asked, voice rough with confusion.

Kaela swallowed hard. "I… I think you do. I think I do too."

His eyes searched hers like they held a map to his own soul.

"I've dreamed of you," he said.

She blinked. "So have I."

A wind rushed past them, stirring the mirrors. The images blurred, then sharpened. One showed them standing just like this—but with a kiss between them, not words.

Kaela looked up at him.

Ezren leaned closer.

Their lips brushed.

A heartbeat away from completion.

Then the Veil screamed.

A sound like the shattering of a thousand bells. Light fractured the space between them. A jagged tear opened in the sky—dark, pulsing, hungry.

Ezren staggered back.

"No—" Kaela reached for him, but the ground beneath his feet gave way.

The Veil pulled him.

"No!" she screamed, lunging forward, catching his wrist.

He held hers, eyes wide with horror.

"Kaela!" he shouted. "Remember me!"

"I'm trying!" she sobbed.

The magic pulled harder.

His grip began to slip.

"Don't let go!"

"I—" His voice broke. "I'm sorry—"

And then he was gone.

The Veil snapped closed.

Kaela collapsed to the stone floor, breath coming in gasps, hand still reaching for a hand no longer there.

The mirrors went dark.

The path behind her began to dissolve.

And a voice echoed from the sky—hers and not hers, layered with time and pain.

"You almost broke the spell. But almost is not enough."

The world tore apart.

And Kaela fell.

The fall wasn't a fall.

It was a plummet through sensation—through time, through memory, through *herself*.

Kaela didn't feel the rush of wind or the weight of her body, only the sickening churn of a thousand fragments spiraling around her. Her skin prickled. Her bones rattled like keys on a ring, each one unlocking something buried deep—moments, lives, losses.

A battlefield under a blood-red moon.

A wedding by starlight.

A knife in her hand, a promise on her lips.

Ezren's voice, whispering her name in a language she didn't know but understood in her marrow.

Her heart screamed through it all—aching, searching—for *him*.

Then, just as suddenly as it had begun, the descent ended.

Kaela hit something soft—moss, maybe, or silk spun from moonlight. She lay there for a moment, trembling, her breath shallow. The air was different again, warm and heady, thick with the scent of night-blooming flowers and magic older than language.

She opened her eyes.

The world had changed again.

She was in a forest—but not one rooted in any realm she knew. The trees shimmered with silver leaves that chimed faintly in the wind, and their trunks curved into impossible spirals. The sky above was a sheet of glass reflecting constellations she didn't recognize. The ground pulsed faintly with a bioluminescent glow, casting her skin in hues of soft blue and amethyst.

The Dreaming Hollow, she thought, the name surfacing from nowhere.

It wasn't in any book she had read. But she *knew* it.

She stood slowly, brushing moss from her coat, the satchel with the tome still slung over her shoulder. The coin Ezren had given her was cool against her chest, hanging from a chain now, though she hadn't remembered putting it there.

"Ezren?" she called, her voice swallowed by the hush.

No answer.

Only the chiming of leaves and the whisper of magic in the wind.

She stepped forward, drawn down a winding path lit by floating motes of silver flame. Her boots made no sound on the mossy earth. Everything around her vibrated with expectation, like the world itself held its breath.

She passed a tree carved with hundreds of names, one atop the other—some in languages she knew, others in scripts she had never seen. One name was etched over and over.

Ezren.

Each time in a different hand.

How many lives...? she wondered, her fingers grazing the

bark.

A branch shifted overhead, and something leapt down into her path.

Kaela stepped back, hand on her dagger.

It was a creature—nearly human, tall and androgynous, clothed in robes of flowing starlight. Its face shimmered, features changing with every blink, impossible to focus on. It tilted its head at her, amused.

"You wear his coin," it said, voice echoing like a bell struck underwater.

"I'm looking for him," Kaela said, standing her ground. "He was taken."

"The Veil does not take. It reveals."

"He fell through."

The creature stepped closer. Its eyes, though unreadable, burned with knowing.

"And so did you."

Kaela gritted her teeth. "Where is he?"

The creature circled her slowly, studying. "You are very close to remembering. That is dangerous."

"I don't care."

"It is not *you* who will pay the price if you choose wrong. It never is."

"What does that mean?"

The creature didn't answer. Instead, it flicked a hand toward the trees. The world bent. Twisted.

And Kaela was *elsewhere*.

The hollow became a ruin—an old cathedral, half-buried in ash and snow. The sky above was crimson, lightning arcing across the heavens. The cathedral's stained glass glowed faintly in the dark, shards of shattered images painting the ground in broken light.

Kaela stood before the altar.

And there he was.

Ezren.

But not as she had last seen him.

This Ezren wore black ceremonial armor, the breastplate scorched and cracked. Blood stained the edge of his mouth. His eyes were wild, desperate—and locked on hers.

"Kaela," he gasped, falling to his knees.

She ran to him, caught him before he collapsed completely.

"I'm here," she whispered, arms wrapping around his body. "I've got you."

"I failed," he said, voice ragged. "They broke through. The spell… I tried to save you…"

His hands clutched her coat, blood smearing across the fabric.

"They're coming," he said. "They'll take everything. You have to—"

Light flared again, and Kaela screamed.

Not in pain.

In *memory*.

The kiss.

Not the one that almost happened.

The one that had.

She saw it clearly now—Ezren, standing in the ruins, one hand cupping her face as magic rose between them like fire. Their lips meeting in a clash of desperation and devotion, a spell blooming in the space between. The binding. The first word of the curse—spoken not to harm, but to protect.

"Tessariel."

A word that meant *forever*.

But nothing was forever.

The kiss had sealed the spell.

And broken them.

Kaela stumbled back as the vision shattered, the cathedral fading into shadow.

The creature stood there again, watching her with calm curiosity.

"You remember," it said.

Kaela's mouth was dry. Her body trembled. "Only pieces."

"You remember enough."

She turned to it, anger rising in her chest. "Why are you showing me this?"

"Because you have not yet chosen."

"Chosen what?"

"To remember fully. Or to forget him forever."

She clenched her fists. "I won't forget him."

The creature raised a brow. "You say that now. But each time, it becomes harder."

Kaela stepped forward. "What happens if I choose to remember?"

"Then the spell unravels."

"And?"

The creature's form flickered. A heartbeat. A sigh. A thousand years in a blink.

"And you both die."

Kaela stared.

"I don't believe you."

"Then why do you hesitate?"

She opened her mouth to argue—but the Hollow had already begun to fade. The forest, the creature, the light—all peeled away like paper curling in flame.

Darkness swallowed her again.

But this time, she didn't fall.

She stood.

In her room.

Alone.

The tome lay open on the desk, a new line scrawled across the page in silver ink.

"The kiss nearly broke the curse. But the curse was made in love—and love demands a price."

Kaela touched her lips.

They still tingled with his memory.

And she swore, then and there, she would pay whatever price was asked.

Because he was worth remembering.

Five

The Spell That Unmakes

The moon was nearly full when Kaela climbed the spiraling steps of the broken observatory. Her breath bloomed in white clouds, dissipating into the midnight air as the wind tugged at her cloak, howling like it mourned some ancient grief. The stone beneath her feet was slick with frost, the railings crumbling beneath her touch. And still she climbed—higher, past broken mechanisms and rusted star-charts, through cobwebs and scattered scrolls left to rot.

At the top, she emerged into a shattered dome of glass and shadow.

Above her, the sky was stitched with stars.

And framed at the center—perfect, luminous—was the moon.

Not yet full.

But close.

The thirteenth eclipse was coming.

The Spells We Wove with Forgotten Words

And with it, the end.

She set the satchel down on a slab of stone that had once been part of the original telescope base, and opened the tome. The binding creaked like a living thing. Pages fluttered against the wind, stopping on their own—settling, she realized, on the spell. The one that had chosen her. Or perhaps *called* her.

Runes crawled across the parchment, alive with violet shimmer. They had shifted since her last reading—grown more defined. The language now curled in symbols too familiar to ignore.

This was not just a spell.

It was a story.

A wound.

A warning.

She reached for the translation notes she had scribbled across parchment and margins, her hands shaking slightly. Her ink was smeared in places—where her tears had landed, or perhaps where the spell had rejected her. But tonight, it welcomed her. Whispered to her.

And she understood.

The spell was a memory-binder.

Crafted in desperation during the final days of the Ember-War, when kingdoms had burned and time itself had frayed. It had been forged by two sorcerers—lovers from rival realms—who knew their names would be erased, their blood hunted, their bond destroyed by the flames of politics and betrayal.

So they created a way to endure.

To survive death.

To anchor themselves in the river of time.

The memory-binder was a tether between souls.

It wove their essence across lives—reincarnating them again

The Spell That Unmakes

and again, binding their magic, memories, and names to one another, so that even if the world forgot them, they would find each other.

But it was not perfect.

And it came at a price.

Each rebirth buried more of who they had been. Their memories became fractured. Their connection dulled. The spell unraveled slowly over the centuries, losing strength.

And now, with the approach of the thirteenth lunar eclipse—the final binding point—the magic would complete its cycle.

If the spell was not undone by that night...

Then the lovers would forget each other.

Forever.

Their names would be purged from all memory. Not just from their minds, but from the very fabric of existence. Every incarnation, every kiss, every sacrifice—

Gone.

As if they had never been.

Kaela's fingers clenched the parchment.

The eclipse was six days away.

Six days until she lost him again.

If she hadn't already.

The Veil Between had pulled him away. Torn them apart just as their kiss had nearly shattered the binding. It had been *so close*. A heartbeat away from remembering everything. From *breaking* the cycle.

She closed her eyes, forcing herself to breathe.

She had to find him.

But more than that—she had to finish decoding the spell. There were fragments still missing. One line remained hidden. Obscured. A single phrase, blurred with static like some stubborn scar.

The Final Unbinding.

She flipped to the next page—bare, save for a single sentence written in shimmering gold.

"To undo the spell, you must relive the moment you first cast it."

Her heart slammed against her ribs.

How?

How could she relive a moment from centuries ago?

Unless…

She looked up, eyes drifting to the moon.

The Veil.

It was the key. It wasn't just a place between realities. It was a memory construct—a living mirror of time's wounds. It responded to the spell. It *had* shown her fragments already.

If she could get back in—*deeper*—she might see the origin of the spell. The night it was spoken.

But she'd need more than willpower.

She'd need *Ezren*.

Only together could they relive it.

And only through shared memory would the spell open.

Suddenly, something shifted in the air behind her.

She turned.

Ezren stood at the edge of the broken dome.

His coat was torn. A new scar traced his cheekbone, and his eyes—Gods, his eyes—burned with sorrow and longing and something like *recognition*.

"Kaela," he said, voice rough with awe.

She didn't move. Couldn't speak.

He crossed the space between them in three long strides, then stopped—hesitating, as if afraid one wrong breath would shatter her.

"Is it you?" he whispered.

She nodded.

Ezren reached up, hand trembling, and brushed her cheek with the back of his fingers. "I saw you in the Hollow. You remembered something. I felt it."

"I remembered *us*," she said softly.

His breath hitched.

She reached into her satchel and pulled out the tome, holding it open between them. He stared at the runes, at the shimmer of gold.

His eyes widened.

"It's the binding," he murmured. "I wrote this. With you."

"I know."

"It was supposed to save us."

"But it's ending," she said. "The spell's breaking down. The eclipse—"

"I know."

A heavy silence fell.

Ezren sank to his knees beside her, staring at the open page. "We've come close before," he said. "Too many times. I felt it—lives where we almost remembered. Almost finished it."

Kaela sat beside him.

"This time," she said, "we don't almost. We *do*."

He looked at her, and his gaze held the weight of centuries. "Are you ready for what it might show us? What we might've done?"

She didn't hesitate. "Yes."

He reached for her hand.

She took it.

And the spell answered.

Light erupted from the page.

Not blinding—but encompassing. Golden strands wrapped around them, lifting them gently from the stones, suspending them between breaths.

The world fell away.

And Kaela opened her eyes—

—to *flames.*

They stood in a war room.

The floor was scorched. The walls cracked.

Banners of two kingdoms hung in tatters—The House of Embers and the Pale Court.

Kaela turned slowly.

There she stood—herself, or another version of herself—clad in dark robes, eyes lined with exhaustion and firelight. Her hands were stained with ink and blood. Her fingers trembled as she hovered over the tome. Beside her, a younger Ezren—hair pulled back, armored, bleeding—watched her with a kind of broken devotion.

"We're out of time," the younger Kaela whispered. "They'll kill us both."

Ezren cupped her face.

"We'll find each other," he said. "We'll always find each other."

Tears welled in her eyes. "Even if we forget?"

"Especially then."

They leaned forward.

And spoke the spell in unison.

Words ancient and sacred, wound with magic, blood, and love.

"Tessariel. Verithan. Sael'mor."

The room trembled. Light surged.

And Kaela and Ezren—the present versions—staggered back

The Spell That Unmakes

as the spell consumed the past.

The memory collapsed.

And they were *back*.

At the observatory.

On the floor.

Shaking.

Kaela clutched Ezren's hand, heart pounding.

"We have to say it," she said. "The Unbinding. Now."

Ezren nodded, voice hoarse. "Together."

They turned to the tome, which now pulsed with white-gold light.

A final line had revealed itself—clear, sharp, waiting.

They began to speak.

Their voices rose, entwined, crackling with power.

The spell bent.

Resisted.

And then—broke.

The runes shattered off the page, dissipating into the wind like ash.

The tome turned to dust.

The coin melted.

Kaela gasped as the pressure lifted from her chest. The pain... it was *gone*.

But Ezren swayed beside her.

"No," she whispered, catching him. "Ezren—?"

His body trembled. His eyes met hers.

"I remember *everything*," he said, voice soft.

And then he collapsed.

The spell was undone.

But the cost had only just begun.

Kaela dropped to her knees, barely catching Ezren's weight before it hit the stone floor. He crumpled against her like something undone, the last threads of strength unraveling from his limbs. His eyes fluttered but didn't close, unfocused, storm-gray now clouded with something darker—something ancient and breaking.

"No, no—Ezren, stay with me." Her voice cracked, sharp and urgent. "Breathe. Look at me."

His lips moved, barely parting. "Kaela…"

"I'm here," she said, clutching him tighter, shaking with the magic that still trembled around them.

All around the observatory, the wind rose in a wild spiral, stirring the dust of the vanished tome into a vortex of light. The remnants of the spell hadn't simply disappeared—they were moving, searching, latching onto something.

Kaela.

Ezren.

Her skin burned with the sudden weight of it—the magic hadn't left. It had transferred.

"Gods," she whispered, watching as a thread of silver light crawled from Ezren's chest into hers, threading through the hollow place behind her heart.

Ezren convulsed once.

Then went still.

For a heartbeat, Kaela thought he had died.

Then he gasped—and the sound cut through her like the slash of a blade. His body arched in her arms, trembling as though something inside him fought to stay tethered. Magic crackled through his veins, veins that shimmered with light under his skin.

"It's too much," he choked. "It's breaking me—"

The Spell That Unmakes

Kaela's hand pressed to his chest, her eyes blazing now, not with fear, but determination. "No. You don't get to leave me. Not now. Not after everything."

His eyes flicked up, meeting hers with what little focus he had left.

"The spell's in you now," he rasped. "That's what it wanted. One of us had to hold the binding… even if it's broken."

"You're not dying," she snapped.

"I'm forgetting."

Her breath caught. "What?"

"It's the curse's backlash," he said, voice fading. "The price for unmaking what was written in blood."

Kaela's hand shook as she cupped his face. "Then I'll anchor you. I'll *make* you remember."

"It's too late."

"No," she growled, drawing him closer. "Not this time."

She pressed her forehead to his. "What do you remember right now? Tell me."

He flinched, as if the act of holding a memory caused him pain. "The war," he whispered. "You. The Hollow. Your name—"

His breath hitched.

"…What's my name, Ezren?"

He didn't answer.

His eyes darted, panicked.

"*Kaela.*" She gripped his jaw, forcing his gaze to meet hers. "My name is Kaela Dorne. You loved me in the ruins. You kissed me under the shattered moon. You followed me across every lifetime and burned down empires for me. Say it."

He closed his eyes, and tears leaked from beneath the lids. But then he whispered, "Kaela."

The Spells We Wove with Forgotten Words

Relief crashed through her like water over stone. She cradled his head, rocked him gently, whispering his name, her name, pieces of memory like incantations.

Outside, the clouds had begun to churn. The sky wept streaks of silver rain as thunder rolled across the highlands. The eclipse had not yet come—but the air already trembled with its anticipation.

Kaela could feel it—something immense approaching, not just in the heavens, but in the fabric of magic itself. The spell they had broken wasn't finished with them.

It had bound them. And now, in its dying breath, it demanded balance.

She pulled Ezren into her lap and closed her eyes. Let the storm take her mind, her soul, the broken mirror of lives shattered and stitched across centuries.

Then she *reached*.

Not with hands—but with *memory*.

She reached into the spell.

And it opened.

It did not fight her now. It showed her what had been hidden.

The Final Unbinding wasn't a phrase.

It was a *place*.

A fragment of magic nestled in a location between time—a shard of what they had once been, sealed at the moment the spell was first cast.

And it pulsed now.

Calling.

Not to end.

But to heal.

To complete the cycle.

Kaela opened her eyes.

The Spell That Unmakes

"I know where we need to go," she said aloud, heart hammering. "The spell's root wasn't just bound to our blood. It was bound to where we cast it."

Ezren stirred weakly. "The ruins..."

"Yes," she said. "The battlefield cathedral. The moment it all began."

"We'll never make it before the eclipse," he murmured.

Kaela's eyes burned with purpose. "We have to."

She helped him to his feet, bracing his weight, half-dragging him across the observatory as the winds screamed louder. With a surge of her remaining power, she snapped her fingers—and the spell circle embedded in her skin flared to life.

A portal formed—violet and gold, ringed with ancient runes and starfire.

Ezren looked at her, eyes wide. "You don't know what going back there will cost."

"I don't care."

She looked back once, at the now-silent observatory, at the ash and dust where the spell had broken.

Then she stepped through.

The ruins were still there.

Beneath the broken cathedral dome, beneath a sky bruised with pre-eclipse shadow, the stones stood just as they had in her vision. Cracked. Burned. Stained with the blood of a war lost to time.

Kaela knelt, Ezren beside her, both of them breathing hard. The portal closed behind them with a final exhale, like the breath of a dying god.

The altar stood ahead.

The very spot where they had once spoken the spell that damned them.

The place that had watched them fall.

They approached together, each step heavy with memory. The moment they crossed the threshold, the air shivered.

Magic woke.

Not hostile.

Not malevolent.

But heavy with grief.

And hope.

Kaela reached into her pocket and withdrew the last piece of the spell—a strip of cloth from her past self's robe. It pulsed with residual magic, faint and fading.

She laid it on the altar.

Ezren's hand joined hers.

Then, together, they spoke.

Not the original binding.

Not the unmaking.

But a new phrase.

A *choice*.

"Let us remember. Let us live. Let the past be truth, not prison."

The ground trembled.

Light rose—pure, white, blinding.

It shot into the sky, where the moon had begun its crossing.

The eclipse began.

And the magic *answered*.

A wind tore through the ruins, lifting their hair, pulling at their clothes. A thousand echoes cried out—every version of them, every life, every kiss and tear and sword drawn in rage.

Kaela saw it all.

Ezren saw her.

And as the moon slid fully into shadow, the spell released

them.

Not in death.

In truth.

Their memories returned—not as fragments, but whole.

Their love—not as legend, but real.

And when the world stilled, and the light faded...

They stood together.

Unbound.

Unbroken.

Alive.

The thirteenth eclipse passed.

And for the first time in a thousand years, Kaela Dorne and Ezren Valen remembered everything.

Six

Whispers of the First Time

The capital's palace loomed before Kaela like a slumbering behemoth. Bathed in moonlight, its walls of obsidian and veined marble shimmered with ethereal glow, casting jagged reflections across the courtyard pools. The spires reached like broken fingers into the clouds, each one a relic of forgotten wars and darker magic.

She shouldn't be here.

Every ward, every rune in the stone warned her away. But Kaela had grown used to walking through the cracks of warnings, had made a habit of slipping into places memory feared to tread.

And tonight, the spell tugged at her again.

Not in panic. Not in pain.

But in *recognition*.

The whispers had started the moment the thirteenth eclipse passed. At first, faint dreams—voices half-heard in sleep, flashes of war banners, the taste of smoke and ash. But then she'd seen the mural in the lower corridors of the Palace Archive—a single crystal panel depicting the Siege of Valeborne Keep.

It had taken her breath.

Not because of the artistry. But because she had seen *herself.*

And Ezren.

On opposite sides of a broken bridge, swords drawn.

Not as lovers.

As enemies.

Betrayers.

The memory wasn't hers. Not fully. But the ache in her chest had flared so violently she nearly collapsed.

The mural had a title carved in silver beneath the crystal:

"The First Fall: House of Embers vs. Pale Court."

That was two nights ago.

Now, with Ezren resting in the safehouse hidden within the Old Quarter, Kaela had returned alone. The spell etched in her veins thrummed in rhythm with the very stone beneath her boots, guiding her deeper into the palace catacombs.

She moved through the winding passageways with practiced silence, her fingertips brushing against walls carved with sigils too old to decipher. Torches flickered to life as she passed, responding not to touch, but to *presence.*

The magic here was ancient.

And it remembered her.

Finally, she came to a wall that was too smooth. Too untouched.

A lie.

She pressed her palm against it.

The stone grew warm.

Then soft.

Then transparent.

A doorway formed—silent, seamless—and beyond it, a spiral stairwell descended into the dark.

Kaela stepped through.

The air turned colder with every step. Her boots rang softly on the stairs, the sound swallowed by thick, enchanted stone. The spiral twisted like the spine of some great serpent, bone-white and gleaming faintly with ghostlight.

Down and down she went, until the air shifted, pressed against her like water, thick with memory.

And then—light.

She emerged into a vaulted chamber so massive it took her breath. The ceiling arched like the inside of a cathedral dome, supported by pillars carved into the shapes of warring kings and queens—each crowned with a broken symbol, half sun, half moon.

At the center of the floor was a crystal dais.

And surrounding it...

Murals.

Etched into massive panes of crystal, arranged in a wide circle, each stood twice Kaela's height. They shimmered faintly, not with magic, but with captured light—moments frozen in time, carved in excruciating detail.

Scenes of war.

Of betrayal.

Of desperate love.

She approached the first.

A battlefield shrouded in ash and blood, two great armies clashing beneath a sky choked in smoke. One banner bore the sigil of the House of Embers—a phoenix bound in chains. The other, the Pale Court's emblem—a crescent moon pierced by a sword.

She moved to the next.

And saw *him.*

Ezren—armor dark with soot and blood, eyes wild, wielding twin blades crackling with red lightning. Beside him, soldiers of shadow and flame.

She turned to the third.

Her own face stared back at her.

But not the scholar. Not the woman who had crawled through ruins and kissed him under stars.

This Kaela wore the ceremonial white armor of the Pale Court, blade in hand, eyes cold as the moons. Behind her, a wall of light and wind-shielded mages bore her banner forward, chanting spells of memory destruction.

They had been *enemies.*

And then she saw the fourth mural.

A meeting at twilight. Ezren and Kaela, cloaked in secrecy, standing between their armies in a forest clearing. No blades. Only hands, clasped.

And the expression on their faces—

Desperation.

Love.

Betrayal.

The next image made her knees buckle.

The siege of a citadel—Ezren's—its walls crumbling under Pale magic. Kaela at the front of the assault. And him, standing on the ramparts, watching her approach with a look not of rage.

But of heartbreak.

The spell in her blood pulsed hard.

The dais in the center of the room lit up.

Kaela rose, drawn to it, her breath shallow.

As she stepped onto the platform, the crystals around her shifted—rotating, rearranging.

And a voice filled the air.

Hers.

Not this life's.

A voice drenched in fire and sorrow.

"Let them call us traitors."

"Let them burn our names from their tomes."

"We will survive the forgetting."

"Because in the end, I will find you again."

"In every life."

Kaela staggered, heart pounding, tears streaming down her face.

The final mural shifted.

It showed the two of them—Ezren and Kaela—bound in arcane chains, back-to-back, as figures from both Houses condemned them. Spells carved from pure memory rained down. Light and flame struck simultaneously.

The Binding.

That was when they had spoken the spell.

Not to save themselves.

But to escape annihilation.

They had chosen *each other* over kingdoms.

Over oaths.

Over everything.

But that choice had cursed them.

Kaela fell to her knees, hand pressed to the dais.

The room trembled.

Runes erupted beneath her palms—golden, pulsing.

Whispers of the First Time

Another voice whispered into the chamber now.

Ezren's.

Soft. Gentle. The voice of another lifetime.

"If we must be forgotten, then let us be forgotten together."

Kaela bowed her head.

And remembered everything.

The first kiss.

The first betrayal.

The first binding.

The first time she had chosen him—knowing it would end everything.

And then, with shaking hands, she reached into her satchel, pulled free a shard of the ruined tome, and placed it onto the glowing dais.

It melted into the stone.

The room lit up.

The murals flared—each image now alive with magic. The figures moved, their memories given breath.

Kaela stood, eyes wide, as her past selves walked those crystal paths. Her past Ezrens met her gaze across lifetimes.

And in every version—

They chose each other.

The spell had never been about survival.

It had been a love letter written across centuries.

Now, it was time to finish it.

The vault doors slammed shut behind her.

And Kaela, surrounded by the echoes of what had been, whispered the truth.

"We were never enemies."

"We were just... in love."

The moment the doors closed, a weight settled on Kaela's chest—not metaphorical, but real, dense as stone. The magic in the chamber condensed, pressing against her lungs and skull like a storm crowding into a bell jar. Her heartbeat echoed in the silence, magnified by the magic-infused air, syncopated with the runes that now lit the floor in concentric circles.

She wasn't alone anymore.

The murals pulsed.

From the walls, light peeled into ribbons. They wove together into shapes—figures rising from the etched crystal panels like ghosts called from sleep. Not illusions. *Impressions.* Residual echoes of memory and soul, summoned not by spell but by blood.

Her blood.

Kaela stepped back instinctively as one of the spectral forms solidified—a younger version of herself, eyes glowing, armor still gleaming from battle. The ghost did not look at her. She looked beyond her, through her, into something deeper.

Another figure formed—Ezren.

Not the man she had kissed beneath moonlight. Not the half-remembered echo that had broken through the spell.

No.

This Ezren wore his rage openly. His eyes were fire, his mouth a cruel line of sorrow. His cloak was torn from war and his hands still dripped with crimson magic. And when he turned to the specter of Kaela, the pain in his face was so vivid Kaela herself flinched.

Their voices—no longer whispers—spoke aloud now, overlapping across space and memory.

"You led them through my gates."

"You let the Ember Prince die."

Whispers of the First Time

"You stole our memories before they could."
"I had to. I had to make sure we remembered *each other*."

Kaela gripped the edge of the dais. "No… no, that's not how it happened."

But the memories paid her no mind. They circled one another—blades drawn but unused. It was clear they could not hurt each other. It was not their way.

But the betrayal had still been real.

Their kingdoms had demanded sacrifice.

And the lovers had sacrificed everything *but* one another.

The younger Kaela raised her palm, and golden runes formed in the air between them. The words etched in blood and love. The first verse of the Binding.

Ezren reached to her, not to stop her, but to join her. His magic—the crimson fire of the Ember line—merged with hers.

The spell ignited.

And the world around them cracked.

Kaela screamed, clutching her head as the memory surged—not around her, but *into* her. She saw the pain. The vow. The desperate, awful love that had cursed them. And she knew, now, why the memory had been buried so deeply.

Because it was *too powerful.*

Too dangerous.

Too raw.

They hadn't cast the Binding to survive.

They had cast it to *escape*.

Kaela stumbled to her knees.

The murals around the room changed again.

They no longer showed wars and betrayals.

They showed aftermaths.

Kaela—alone in a monastery, studying languages that hurt

to remember.

Ezren—drifting through time, faces changed, lives blurred.

Kaela—burning a kingdom to the ground for a reason she no longer understood.

Ezren—watching her die in a dozen lifetimes, powerless to stop it.

Kaela—finding him again, again, again. Always a step too late.

And in each iteration, a moment.

A kiss.

A spark.

A pull.

The spell was not a chain.

It was a *path*.

They had not been punished.

They had been given the only gift they could have salvaged from the ruins of what they destroyed.

Each other.

But the time was almost over.

The thirteenth eclipse had passed.

And without the final verse, the spell's memory would dissolve. The magic would dissipate. The path would end.

Kaela rose, slowly.

She walked to the center of the dais where the glowing runes waited. Her breath trembled as she reached into her satchel and pulled out the final piece she'd held in secret.

A single feather—silver-black, streaked with firelight.

Ezren's feather. From a life she'd nearly forgotten.

She placed it at the center of the sigil.

And whispered the last line of the Binding.

Not from the tome.

Not from memory.

From her soul.

"If time is fire, then let us burn together."

The room exploded in silence.

Every mural shattered at once—glass shards flying, bursting into light, cascading through the room like starlight made solid. The echoes screamed, not in agony, but in *release.* Chains snapped. Wards collapsed. The ghosts of past lives dissolved into warmth, into gold.

Kaela stood at the center of it all, arms open, tears running down her face.

Then—

A step.

A voice.

"Kaela."

She turned.

Ezren stood just inside the threshold, breathless, his skin aglow with the residual magic of the broken spell.

"You felt it," she whispered.

"I followed it."

He stepped toward her.

She didn't move.

He reached her in two strides.

His hands cradled her face, reverent, aching.

"You remembered it all," he said.

"So did you."

"Then let me say it this time," he murmured. "Not for magic. Not to bind. Just because it's true."

He leaned in, and the kiss was quiet.

Not like the desperate ones of before.

Not like the stolen ones behind enemy lines or the forbidden ones beneath eclipsed moons.

This kiss was gentle.

And *earned*.

And when they broke apart, the room was gone.

The vault had dissolved.

Only the two of them remained, standing beneath the roots of the world, beneath stars that had once watched them destroy their kingdoms for love.

"I don't want to lose you again," Kaela whispered.

"You won't," Ezren said. "Not this time."

A pause.

Then—

"Do you hear them?" he asked.

She listened.

In the distance—so faint, so far—a new voice was whispering.

A future.

Unwritten.

But waiting.

Seven

The Pact of Ash and Flame

The wind that swept the northern edge of the Blackward Mountains wasn't wind at all—it was breath. Hot, ancient, restless. It moaned through the jagged crevices like a beast caged beneath the stone. The path Ezren took curled upward along a cliff face, its edges scorched black, every foothold crumbling into embers with each step.

He walked alone, his cloak whipped behind him by the furnace winds, boots searing against a path most sorcerers avoided for good reason. The air here smelled of sulfur and forgotten curses. The stone was laced with obsidian veins that pulsed red in a heartbeat rhythm, echoing something buried far below.

The Searing Archive.

A place not marked on any map, and spoken of only in half-muttered tales by mages who knew the cost of curiosity.

But Ezren had no room left for hesitation.

Kaela's memories were flooding back. The spell was unraveling. The past was no longer a distant storm—it was the ground beneath their feet, cracking open. If they didn't retrieve the lost verse of the Binding before the remnants of the spell devoured what remained of their identities, there would be nothing left to hold them together. Not even love.

He pressed his hand to the mark on his chest—a sigil burned there during their last encounter with the Veil Between. It pulsed faintly, a reminder of the power still tethered to their shared past. Of the vow he had broken once, long ago.

He would not break it again.

The mouth of the Archive appeared ahead—a jagged fissure in the rock that leaked smoke instead of shadow. The opening breathed, pulling heat inward, then exhaling ash like some sleeping colossus. Ezren paused at the threshold, squinting into the glowing dark.

Then he stepped inside.

The moment he crossed the threshold, the temperature spiked.

Sweat slicked his back within seconds. His skin prickled with awareness. Every inch of him was under scrutiny, though he saw no eyes, heard no voices. But he felt them—watching.

The Flame Spirits.

Guardians of the Archive, protectors of spells too dangerous to destroy, too sacred to forget. They did not speak in words. They spoke in *heat*.

Ezren descended the slope, flanked by walls that dripped with molten crystal and ancient iron. His boots sizzled where they touched the floor. The path forked in unnatural directions—none straight, none logical. Time and space bent here, reshaped by the residual magic of a thousand flame-etched memories.

The Archive was not a place.

It was a *being*.

And it had awakened.

He came to a stone platform suspended over a lake of fire, the surface bubbling with liquefied memory. A bridge of blackened bone led to the heart of the chamber, where a pedestal stood—glowing.

Upon it: a single scroll.

Wrapped in gold-twined ashleaf, sealed with a sigil Ezren recognized instantly.

Kaela's crest.

But older.

Twisted.

This wasn't her crest as a scholar, or even as a soldier of the Pale Court. It was the sigil of her original bloodline—one that had been erased from every record, consumed by the Pact that created the Binding.

His hand reached for it.

The heat flared.

From the molten lake rose the guardians—bodies forged of pure flame, eyes burning blue within skulls of smoke. They didn't move like humans. They *floated,* shifting in and out of shape with each breath. The largest approached, its flame pulsing in time with Ezren's heartbeat.

It spoke—not in words, but *pressure,* felt directly in his bones.

"He who seeks the root of the spell must pay the cost of remembrance."

Ezren braced his stance, sweat pouring down his temples. "Name the cost."

The fire-being leaned closer, its heat blistering the air

between them.

"Your skin has known no flame. Your blood has passed through battle unburned. You carry the mark of an ancient immunity—bestowed by the first bond between your soul and hers."

"I know."

"Give it up."

Ezren's stomach clenched.

His resistance to magical fire wasn't just a talent. It was the last inheritance from the Binding—a shield forged by the love he and Kaela had sealed with blood and vow. Surrendering it meant pain. Exposure. Vulnerability.

But more than that—

It meant *trust*.

Because if Kaela failed... if she forgot again... if this time was like all the others...

He would burn.

Forever.

But Ezren had already made his choice, long before stepping into this place.

"I accept," he said.

The fire-being extended one hand, and flame coiled from its palm, a ribbon of molten light that wrapped around Ezren's chest, tightening.

Pain bloomed instantly.

Not physical—not yet.

This was soul-deep.

Every memory tied to Kaela—the warmth of her laughter, the light of her defiance, the fire of her kiss—ignited behind his ribs. The ribbon pressed inward, searing the immunity from his blood, drawing it out in threads of light that floated to the ceiling, absorbed by the Archive.

Ezren fell to one knee, gasping, as the bond broke.

And for the first time since their spell was cast lifetimes ago, *he felt the heat.*

The spirits parted.

The scroll floated from the pedestal and hovered before him, unrolling mid-air.

Ezren forced himself to stand.

His vision blurred from the pain, but the words burned themselves into his mind—runic, winding, alive. They shifted even as he read them, as though they were remembering themselves with his every breath.

It was the missing verse.

The first invocation of the Pact of Ash and Flame.

A counterbinding—*not* to break the spell, but to finish what had been interrupted centuries ago.

The final truth of the Binding was not preservation.

It was *transformation.*

They had never meant to return to who they were. The spell wasn't a cycle.

It was a bridge.

One life to the next.

One truth to the other.

Ezren read the final line aloud.

As the words left his mouth, the Archive trembled.

The spirits bowed.

And the lake of fire stilled, as if the Archive itself had exhaled.

The scroll sealed itself once more and landed in his outstretched hand.

His skin was already blistering from the heat, and his magic no longer protected him. But the price had been paid.

Ezren turned, clutching the scroll, and made his way back up the path. Each step burned, each breath scorched his lungs. But he did not stop.

Because he saw her face in every flicker of flame.

Kaela.

Waiting.

And now, finally, he could give her what she'd been searching for.

Not just the truth.

But the *choice*.

To end the spell on their terms.

To rewrite their fate—not as a cycle of loss…

But as a legacy of fire.

Together.

Ezren didn't remember collapsing.

He only remembered waking up to the taste of iron on his tongue and the weight of flame pressing down on his chest.

Pain was no longer a distant echo. It was *everywhere*.

It lived in the cracks of his fingers where fire had kissed flesh too long. It burned behind his ribs where magic had once flowed effortlessly, now reduced to embers. The ground beneath him throbbed with heat, and the cave walls twisted in his vision, pulsing in and out of shape like molten glass.

But he had the scroll.

Fingers blackened with soot clutched it tightly against his chest, even as agony radiated from every nerve.

The air in the Searing Archive shifted again.

Not with flame this time, but with *intention*.

The flame spirits had receded, satisfied with the price extracted. Their glowing figures hung in the air like distant stars, their heat subdued. One of them drifted toward him, its form less defined now, more smoke than light. It hovered silently for a long moment.

Then, without warning, it extended a single glowing hand toward him.

Ezren tensed.

But instead of searing him again, the spirit pressed two fingers gently to his temple.

A cool rush surged through his body—not healing, but *clarity.*

A memory not his own unfolded in the space between heartbeats.

Not from a past life.

From hers.

Kaela, long ago—standing in the ruins of a tower during the last days of the Ember War. Her hand pressed to a burning sigil on the wall. Her voice hoarse from battle. Her eyes wide with awe and horror as she whispered the lines of the spell for the first time, her voice cracking under the weight of it.

"Let fire remember where words forget."

"Let ash bind what time unravels."

"Let him follow me through flame."

Ezren gasped as the memory burned into his own.

He stumbled to his feet, limbs shaking, heart racing with renewed urgency. Kaela hadn't just cast the spell for protection.

She had done it for *him.*

To pull him through lifetimes.

To *anchor* him.

He understood now.

The pact wasn't punishment. It was a vow.

They had rewritten the rules of fate not out of desperation—but out of love so furious it had dared to challenge time itself.

He staggered toward the exit of the Archive, every movement pain-wracked. The path twisted around him, blurred by smoke and memory, but the scroll burned steady in his hand like a lodestar.

The moment he crossed the threshold, cool night air slapped him across the face.

Ezren fell to his knees just outside the fissure, gulping down mouthfuls of clean air, shaking uncontrollably. The fire had scorched his body, yes—but his soul had been the true battlefield.

He didn't rise for a long time.

Instead, he sat beneath the fractured moon, letting the breeze wrap around his wounds, listening to the wind hum with the final syllables of the spell.

Kaela would feel it. Somewhere, across the span of land and spell and soul—she would *know*.

He had it.

He had *everything*.

But there was something else, something the flame had not demanded but he now understood:

The truth would only matter if she *chose* to speak the final word with him.

The pact could not be completed by one soul.

It had to be shared.

He forced himself to stand again, each step down the mountain heavier than the last. The scroll pulsed against his chest, a heartbeat not his own, and he realized—

It wasn't the spell's heart anymore.

It was Kaela's.

And now he had to bring it back to her.

Back to the one who had started the fire.

The Pact of Ash and Flame

Back to the one he would burn beside.

Kaela was already pacing when he arrived at the threshold of the safehouse.

She threw open the door the moment she felt his presence through the bond—raw and newly exposed since the immunity had burned away. Her eyes locked on his form, and a gasp tore from her lips.

"Ezren—"

He was pale, his skin marked with blisters and smoke tattoos. His coat hung in tatters. But he was upright.

Alive.

And smiling.

In his hand, wrapped in cloth, he held the scroll.

Kaela's breath caught.

"You found it," she whispered.

He nodded, stepping inside, wobbling once before she caught him.

"I gave them everything," he murmured. "And they gave us the end of the story."

She helped him to the table, easing him into a chair, cradling his ruined hands in hers. "What did they make you give?"

Ezren met her gaze.

"The fire immunity," he said. "The last gift from the first Binding. It's gone."

She paled. "You'll burn if—"

"If we fail," he said softly, "I know."

She held his hand tighter. "Then we won't."

Ezren unraveled the scroll carefully.

Golden ink shimmered across the page in three interwoven tongues—one for time, one for memory, one for *choice*.

Kaela read it once.

The Spells We Wove with Forgotten Words

Twice.

Her eyes widened. "This isn't just the final verse."

"It's the truth," Ezren said. "What we really meant to do."

She looked at him, wonder blooming across her features.

"You remember it, don't you?" she asked. "All of it."

"I do."

"So do I."

A silence fell between them.

Not uncomfortable.

Holy.

Then Kaela placed her hand over his on the scroll.

She leaned in, forehead pressed to his.

And together, they whispered:

"Let fire remake us."

"Let love bind freely."

"Let us choose one another… even now."

The scroll burst into light.

And the pact—

The true pact—

Was sealed.

Not by flame.

But by *will*.

And the world, once again, began to change.

Eight

A Memory Shared

The wind had shifted.

Kaela could feel it long before she saw the crest of the hill, before the trees parted and the half-crumbled watchtower emerged from the mist. The air shimmered with tension—like the breath before a scream, or the heartbeat before a spell ruptures. The scent of wildfire clung faintly to the breeze, carried down from the mountain pass where Ezren had vanished days ago.

She quickened her pace.

Each step cracked dry leaves beneath her boots, her satchel bumping rhythmically against her hip. The scroll—Ezren's scroll—was gone, vanished in golden light after they had spoken the final verse. But the bond it had reawakened between them hadn't gone dormant. It *pulsed*.

He was here.

Alive.

But not whole.

She reached the clearing just as the first stars began to pierce the twilight sky, and there he was—leaning against a broken column, his back to her, cloak fluttering slightly. His figure was motionless, but Kaela could feel the static in the air around him. Like his very body was struggling to stay tethered to the now.

Her breath caught. "Ezren."

He didn't turn.

She stepped closer.

"Ezren, it's me—"

His head lifted.

She stopped.

His face was pale, drawn—his eyes bloodshot and shadowed—but he smiled.

"Kaela," he rasped.

She crossed the distance and fell to her knees in front of him, cupping his face before she even thought to hesitate. His skin was fever-hot beneath her palms.

But he didn't pull away.

Their eyes locked.

And in the stillness between their breaths—*it happened.*

The memory slammed into them both like a lightning strike through a mirror.

One moment they were kneeling in the broken present.

The next—they stood beneath a sky bursting with falling stars, golden trails lighting the air in trembling silence.

Kaela gasped as her head tipped back.

Ezren stood before her, younger, unscarred, his hair loose, his eyes alight with wonder and something deeper.

They were alone in a wide field of pale firegrass, the stalks

A Memory Shared

glowing faintly under the meteor rain. The sky burned violet and silver.

And Kaela laughed.

She could feel it—not just see it, *feel* it—the wind in her hair, the weight of a new blade at her back, the warmth of Ezren's hand in hers.

They kissed.

Slow, then desperate. Mouths finding each other as the sky shattered above them.

And when they broke apart, Kaela said something.

But the words—*the language*—weren't her own.

She didn't *know* them. Couldn't speak them now.

Yet they passed through her lips as if they'd been carved into her soul.

Ezren answered her in the same tongue.

A vow.

A promise.

A pact.

Then—

Pain.

Sharp. Sudden.

Kaela screamed, staggering back as the memory was ripped from her mind like flesh from bone.

Her knees struck the ground.

Ezren convulsed beside her, clutching his head. Blood ran from his nose. His magic flared out of control—a burst of heat and light that scorched the grass in a wide radius around them.

Kaela crawled to him, grabbed his shoulders. "Ezren—"

He opened his eyes, dazed. "That was us."

"I know."

"We were—" He choked on the words. "We spoke the vow."

"But it's gone," she whispered. "I can't remember what I said."

"Neither can I."

Their breathing was ragged. Blood smeared his lip; sweat plastered Kaela's hair to her temples.

"It hurt," he said. "Why did it hurt?"

Kaela sat back on her heels, staring up at the stars—the same stars that had once watched them fall in love, now distant and cruel.

"The spell's broken," she murmured. "But the vow we made—"

"It still holds," Ezren finished, horror dawning in his voice. "And it's not done with us."

The shared memory wasn't benign.

It was a *trigger*.

And it was getting worse.

Every time they touched, every moment of clarity, the past clawed its way forward—and their bodies suffered for it.

"I thought the scroll finished it," Kaela said, staring at her trembling hands.

"It did," Ezren replied. "But we never undid the *vow*."

She looked at him.

"You mean…"

He nodded, swallowing hard. "There's another piece. A hidden anchor. A vow we made in a tongue older than the spell. We didn't just bind our memories. We sealed something else."

Kaela shook her head slowly. "We were too desperate. We didn't trust the spell alone."

"We made a second promise," Ezren said.

"To each other."

"And now… it's buried."

A Memory Shared

"Worse," Kaela said. "It's *killing* us."

A silence fell.

Somewhere in the forest, something cracked—distant and ancient, like stone shifting in its grave.

They stood slowly, limbs shaking, eyes locked.

Kaela reached for his hand again.

Ezren hesitated—but let her.

When their fingers touched, the memory surged again.

This time a battlefield.

Kaela over a wounded Ezren, holding a blade over both their hearts.

"Do it," he had whispered.

"No," she'd said. "Not yet."

The memory shattered before the blood could fall.

They broke contact.

Both staggered.

"It's happening faster now," Kaela gasped.

"It's not just memory anymore," Ezren said. "It's unraveling."

Kaela looked toward the sky.

"Then we need to find the vow," she said. "Wherever it's hidden. We need to finish what we started."

Ezren nodded grimly. "Before it finishes us."

They stood in silence as the stars pulsed overhead.

Their hands didn't touch.

Not this time.

Because love had never been the danger.

It was the *promise* of forever they had to survive.

The forest pressed in on them.

Even in the dark, it seemed to breathe—branches rustling not with wind, but with something deeper. Sentience. Awareness.

As though the woods had witnessed too many spells, too many oaths whispered into its moss-draped hollows. Now it listened again.

Kaela and Ezren walked in silence, side by side but deliberately apart, careful not to brush shoulders or graze fingertips. Neither trusted what might happen if they did.

Their last touch had almost pulled them apart from the inside out.

"I don't remember learning a language like that," Kaela said at last, her voice quiet. "The one from the memory. I've studied hundreds—Ancient Lorian, the Root Dialect, even broken Tethyran. But this…"

"It was older than language," Ezren replied. "It didn't come from books. It came from *us*."

"A soul-tongue?"

He nodded. "Some magics don't translate. They're felt, not learned. Spoken from the bones."

They passed beneath a stone arch swallowed by roots. Ahead, the terrain sloped downward, revealing a clearing bathed in silver moonlight. A broken circle of standing stones lay at its heart—tall, cracked monuments engraved with glyphs that shimmered faintly in the dark.

Ezren stopped just short of the circle.

"This is it," he said, his voice ragged. "This is where we made it."

Kaela's eyes widened. "The vow?"

He nodded once.

She stepped toward the circle—and staggered back as the air turned thick, viscous, thrumming with power.

The stones reacted to her presence. Runes lit one by one in a slow cascade, as if testing her. Accepting her.

A Memory Shared

Ezren followed, and the reaction doubled—runes flaring brighter, the ground pulsing beneath their boots.

"Gods," Kaela breathed. "It remembers us."

The ring was more than a monument.

It was a *vault*.

But not of stone.

Of *promise*.

Kaela stepped inside the circle.

Ezren followed.

And the past struck them both like lightning down a shared spine.

The memory was full this time.

No gaps.

No pain.

Only presence.

Kaela stood on this very spot, in a different body, different armor, her hands cut and bleeding from battle. Ezren faced her, half-draped in the cloak of his fallen commander, the firelight around them casting gold into his hair.

They were both shaking.

Behind them, the sounds of war still echoed—distant screams, steel on steel. The end of the Ember War. The collapse of the Pale Court. All around them, kingdoms crumbled.

And in the center of it all, they stood beneath a sky streaked with the afterbirth of spells too strong for the world to contain.

"We can't win," Kaela had said.

"No," Ezren had agreed. "But we can *remember*."

She had pulled something from her satchel—two shards of obsidian, each etched with their blood and a single rune.

A rune older than any known language.

She pressed one to his heart.

He pressed one to hers.

The stones fused into their skin like ink poured into fire.

And then they spoke—not in common tongue, not in any tongue of scholars or spellwrights—but in the soul-language.

Their voices layered. Overlapping. Too many syllables. Too much emotion.

A vow.

Ezren took her hands.

"If time forgets us…"

Kaela's lips moved with his.

"…let our souls remember."

"If magic breaks…"

"…let our fire bind."

"If love dies…"

"…let it burn again."

They kissed.

The memory flared white-hot—

And they were back in the clearing.

On their knees.

Screaming.

The vow had returned in full.

And with it, *repercussions.*

Kaela clutched her chest, her pulse a war drum in her ears. Her skin rippled with magic scars that hadn't been there moments ago. Runes shimmered down her arms, forming and fading in the same breath.

Ezren collapsed beside her, blood trickling from his ears, his eyes wild.

"It's *still active*," he gasped. "All this time—"

Kaela turned to him. "We didn't seal the vow. We *ignited* it."

The rune-bond hadn't been a spell.

A Memory Shared

It had been a *living promise,* made without understanding the consequences.

And now, with the Binding broken, the vow was unraveling its final purpose.

Kaela's vision blurred. The stones around them shimmered, their glyphs syncing with her heartbeat.

"Ezren…" she said weakly.

"I know."

"We have to end it. Not break it—*release* it."

"How?"

Kaela looked at him, really looked at him.

"I think we have to do it the same way we made it."

"Together?"

She nodded.

Another silence.

Then Ezren reached for her hand—slowly, painfully. Every inch of movement made his body twitch with searing heat. But he didn't stop.

Their fingers met.

The pain was instant. White-hot.

But they held on.

And spoke.

Together.

Their voices rose—not with words of power, but with words of *choice.*

No longer soul-chained.

No longer desperate.

No longer binding.

"We remember now."

"We choose each other—

—freely."

The vow reacted.

A vortex of golden light burst from the center of the circle, rising into the sky like a reversed flame. The stones cracked and splintered. The runes shattered. The ancient spell—the vow that had hunted them across lifetimes—*dissolved.*

And in its place—

Peace.

True, bone-deep silence.

Ezren collapsed into Kaela's arms.

Their magic didn't flare.

Their memories didn't fade.

Their hearts beat as one.

Still.

Human.

And finally, *free.*

Nine

The Curse Unfolds

The town of Merrowin had once been known for its bells.

Silver-throated, intricately forged, hung high in the towers of sandstone chapels. Every morning they had rung together, a chorus of sound that echoed over wheat fields and forest edges, a heartbeat of memory and rhythm for the people who lived there.

But today, the bells did not ring.

Today, the streets were quiet.

And no one remembered why.

Kaela stood at the edge of the town square, boots coated in dust, her cloak stained with ash from the burning fields they'd passed on their journey. She kept one hand on the hilt of her blade—not because of danger she could see, but because of what she *couldn't*.

The people of Merrowin moved like marionettes cut free

of their strings. Listless. Lost. Children wandered without mothers. Old men wept in corners, faces slack with confusion. Names had vanished. Faces no longer carried meaning. Some villagers had simply stopped speaking altogether.

Ezren stood beside her, face pale. His hand twitched at his side, sparks of unstable magic snapping across his fingertips.

"It's worse than I thought," he said.

Kaela nodded, jaw tight. "It's not just forgetting. It's *erasure*."

They'd seen the first signs on the outskirts. A farm without tools. A cottage without doors. People sitting still in the grass as though waiting for a name to pass their lips and remind them who they were. But here, in the heart of the town, the spell had *nested*.

And it was spreading.

Kaela turned to one of the villagers—a young girl, perhaps thirteen, seated on the edge of the fountain. Her dress was stained with ink, and her hands trembled in her lap. A name was stitched into her collar.

"Liora."

Kaela knelt in front of her.

"Hello," she said gently. "Do you know where your family is?"

The girl blinked.

"My... what?"

"Your family," Kaela repeated. "Parents? Siblings?"

The girl's lips parted.

Then closed again.

"I... I don't know what that word means."

A chill lanced through Kaela's spine.

Ezren stepped forward, his voice low. "What's the last thing you remember, Liora?"

The Curse Unfolds

"I was... I was writing," she said slowly, as though pulling the words from water. "There was a book. A red book. And... and someone took it. Someone with a face I couldn't see."

Ezren and Kaela exchanged a look.

"A red book?" Kaela asked.

Liora nodded. "It glowed."

Kaela stood, her hands curling into fists.

"It's not just affecting people," she said. "It's pulling from the spell. The Binding. Our memories are *anchors*—but now the magic's unmoored, it's dragging everyone down with us."

Ezren turned, scanning the horizon. "The vow is broken. But the Binding... it wasn't isolated to us. We *wove it through time.* Through the world. This plague is it unraveling."

Kaela whispered, "And it's taking everything with it."

A sharp scream cut through the air.

They spun as a man staggered into the square, clawing at his face. His eyes were wide with panic, blood streaking down from torn skin.

"Make it stop!" he sobbed. "Make the voices stop! They keep asking me who I am—I don't KNOW—I don't KNOW!"

He collapsed in a heap, sobbing into his arms.

No one moved to help him.

Because they didn't *remember* how.

Ezren rushed to the man's side, casting a gentle stabilizing ward. His magic flickered with resistance—less effective here, dampened by the chaotic pulse of the unraveling spell.

"This town's at the center of a memory fracture," he said. "There must be a source."

Kaela glanced at the church tower, where the largest of the bells once hung. "If the curse is radiating from something, it would've nested in a place of rhythm. Routine. That's how spells anchor—through repetition."

They made their way through the town, past shuttered windows and doors sealed not with locks, but runes smeared in ash. Magic-users had tried to resist, once.

They had failed.

Inside the chapel, dust hung in thick columns of sunlight. The pews were overturned, the altar smashed. The bell rope had been severed, frayed ends swinging gently in still air.

And at the center of the dais, where the altar once stood, lay a circle of scorched stone.

Within it—a sigil.

Ezren hissed.

Kaela knelt.

The runes weren't familiar. Not *now*.

But her bones remembered them.

"It's part of the original Binding," she whispered.

"It's feeding on place," Ezren said. "Memory etched into the world. This town existed on pattern. It's feeding on that until there's nothing left."

Kaela touched the sigil.

Her vision *snapped*.

She stood in a burning field, a book cradled in her arms.

Not *her*. Not now.

A version of her.

Another life.

This Kaela wore red, her face lined with soot and starlight. Soldiers burned around her. She whispered into the pages, desperate, trembling.

Ezren stood behind her, blood dripping from his hands.

"They're coming," he'd said.

"We're not ready," she'd replied.

The Curse Unfolds

But she opened the book anyway.

And read the first line of the spell that would tether them to the world.

As she did, the flames devoured the field.

And the spell reached through time.

Kaela reeled back with a gasp, her body crashing into Ezren's as the vision broke.

His hands caught her, steadied her.

"I saw it," she whispered. "The first time it spread. We *used* the towns. The people. Their memories *became* the threads."

Ezren's jaw clenched. "That's why it's unraveling now. Because we're no longer part of it."

Kaela nodded.

"The Binding needs us to complete the circuit. Without us—it collapses. And everything it touched collapses with it."

"We need to contain it," Ezren said. "Stop it from reaching the capital."

Kaela stood, drawing a deep breath.

"And to do that, we have to burn it out."

Ezren blinked. "You want to destroy the anchor?"

"Yes," she said. "If we leave the root untouched, this won't stop. It'll spread city by city, until every name, every face, every *history* is ash."

Ezren stared at the sigil.

"We'll need a seal," he said. "A counter-surge strong enough to isolate the fracture."

Kaela looked at him. "We use the same thing that made it: a memory."

He frowned. "A shared one?"

She nodded. "One we both hold. One strong enough to *burn.*"

The Spells We Wove with Forgotten Words

His throat worked. "Which one?"

She didn't have to answer.

They both knew.

The kiss under falling starlight.

The first vow.

The beginning of the Binding.

Kaela stepped into the center of the sigil. "Join me."

Ezren hesitated.

Then stepped in.

The air turned to fire.

Runes lit beneath their feet. The stone burned white-gold.

They clasped hands.

Pain rushed through their bodies—violent, searing, more intense than anything they'd felt before. Their skin blistered. Their vision swam.

But they didn't let go.

Together, they closed their eyes—

—and remembered.

The kiss.

The stars.

The whispered vow in a forgotten tongue.

Not as curse.

As *promise.*

As *love.*

The spell ignited.

The sigil shrieked and *shattered.*

A column of fire burst from the chapel roof into the sky.

And then—

Silence.

Not empty.

Clean.

The Curse Unfolds

Ezren collapsed.

Kaela caught him, cradling his head.

Outside, the bells of Merrowin rang for the first time in weeks.

Slow. Uneven. But real.

Kaela closed her eyes.

And for the first time in days, her name didn't ache to remember.

The bells rang like they were relearning how.

Staggered, uncertain, some cracked and hollow—but they rang. And the sound moved like ripples through still water, touching the edges of Merrowin, then moving outward into the dark beyond.

Kaela cradled Ezren's head in her lap beneath the broken roof of the chapel, where smoke and star-glow still lingered like breath. The fire had left no ash, only scorched stone and the ghost of something ancient, something finally letting go.

Ezren's eyes fluttered open.

She didn't speak. Just pressed her palm to his cheek, her thumb brushing away blood and soot.

"I thought we wouldn't make it," he murmured, voice rough as gravel.

Kaela exhaled a breath she hadn't realized she was holding. "We almost didn't."

They sat there in the hush, the air heavy with magic spent, the way a body feels after fever breaks. The world outside was shifting—Kaela could feel it in the ground beneath them, in the threads of time that had loosened and now tried to stitch themselves back together.

Ezren slowly pushed himself upright. His hands shook.

"Look," he said hoarsely.

Kaela turned her gaze to the open chapel doors.

The villagers were gathering.

They stepped into the square like people emerging from dream. No longer aimless, no longer blank. They reached for each other—slowly at first, cautiously. Then with growing urgency. A man fell to his knees and cried a woman's name. A child threw herself into her mother's arms.

One by one, names returned.

Faces found meaning.

The Binding had released its hold.

But not without scars.

Kaela stood slowly, limbs trembling. The magic they'd called forth had drained her to the marrow. She could still feel the memory they'd summoned—the kiss, the vow—reverberating behind her ribs like an echo that hadn't finished fading.

Ezren rose beside her, unsteady but standing.

His expression was unreadable as he looked out at the town. At what they had almost lost.

"We used them," he said softly.

Kaela looked at him.

"We used *everyone*," he continued. "We built our spell through their lives, their routines, their thoughts… all to preserve what we didn't want to lose."

"It wasn't just selfish," she said quietly. "It was desperate."

"That doesn't make it right."

"No. But now we understand it. And we can stop it."

Ezren turned to her, his eyes darker than she remembered—burned clean of the glamour that once softened him. "What if we can't?"

"We just did," she said. "One town at a time if we have to."

The Curse Unfolds

"But the curse isn't done."

She didn't deny it.

Because even now, beyond Merrowin, she could *feel* it. A tremor moving across the land—not just magic but *time,* slipping out of alignment. The vow was gone. But the spell's echoes had been woven through entire regions.

Cities built on repetition.

Cathedrals whose prayers had been looped into the threads of the Binding.

Libraries whose memories had been used to anchor Kaela and Ezren to *this world.*

They weren't just unraveling history.

They were unraveling *reality.*

Ezren touched her shoulder gently. "We'll need to go to the Source."

Kaela looked at him sharply. "You mean…"

He nodded.

"The Memory Vaults beneath Caladris."

Kaela swallowed.

Caladris had once been the capital of recorded magic. The last seat of the Lore Houses. Abandoned now, after the war. Buried under stone and ruin.

And under the first copies of every known spell in the realm.

Including the earliest records of the Binding.

"If the curse is spreading," Ezren said, "that's where it'll root next. If it hasn't already."

Kaela nodded. "Then we go."

They stepped from the chapel together.

The town was alive again. Dimly. Like a candle relit after being long snuffed out. But they could already feel the instability in the threads. This wasn't over.

Not yet.

As they passed the villagers, many stared at them. Some recognized them. Most did not. But there was no fear in their eyes—only awe, and something deeper.

Gratitude.

Kaela paused at the edge of the square.

A girl stood watching her—Liora, her name stitched again at her collar.

She smiled.

Kaela smiled back.

Then she and Ezren turned toward the mountains, toward Caladris, toward the wound that had never really closed.

And behind them, the bells of Merrowin tolled once more—clearer this time.

Remembering.

Ten

Love in a Loop

The ruins of Caladris rose like bone from the dust.

Kaela paused at the edge of the crumbled path, boots sinking into ash. Wind tugged at her cloak, whispering through the hollow spires with a sound like breath caught in a dying throat. Somewhere below, the Memory Vaults waited, buried deep beneath collapsed academies and forgotten temples, beneath the last city that had dared to catalogue every known spell in the world.

Ezren stood beside her, silent.

They didn't speak as they moved through the broken gates, once plated with living silver. Now, vines had claimed them— veins of dark ivy curling across the bent and rusted sigils of the Lore Houses. Statues of long-dead mages loomed over the path, their eyes cracked and blind, as if unwilling to witness what the city had become.

They passed beneath archways that once rang with incantations, into halls choked with the dust of abandoned knowledge. The walls breathed old magic—restless, fractured. Memory bled from the stones in threads Kaela could almost see.

This place remembered everything.

Every word ever spoken in its halls.

Every spell ever written.

Every name ever burned into its walls.

Even hers.

Even his.

Kaela's hand brushed against a pillar etched in runes. Her fingers caught on a shallow groove—barely visible. She leaned in, heart thudding.

Kaelaria Dorne.

Not carved by stonemason's chisel.

But by her own hand.

She didn't remember doing it.

Not in this life.

But the sight of it made her dizzy.

"Here," Ezren said softly, his voice echoing like a ghost. He gestured to a collapsed corridor to the right, half-covered in debris.

Kaela followed him into the dark.

They lit no torches. The Vaults hated open flame. But their magic shimmered faintly in the dark—enough to guide them down the twisting stairwells and crumbling ramps that spiraled deeper beneath the city.

Time didn't flow normally here.

And memory had no boundaries.

They walked for what felt like hours. Or minutes. Or lifetimes.

Until they reached it.

A door with no handle.

No lock.

Only a smooth sheet of onyx, embedded with a single palm-shaped indent.

Kaela stepped forward before Ezren could. Her heart told her it had to be her.

She pressed her hand to the stone.

Warmth.

Then resistance.

Then a sound—like glass breaking underwater.

The door opened.

The chamber beyond was circular, vast, and quiet.

Bookshelves curved along the walls like ribs, reaching into the dark beyond the lanternless dome. The floor was tiled in white stone, each slab etched with a name. Some glowed faintly. Others pulsed like hearts.

Kaela walked to the center, where a pedestal stood—unassuming. Upon it rested a single book, leatherbound, cracked, its cover blackened with soot.

She knew it instantly.

Because her name was on the spine.

Not "Kaelaria."

But *all of them.*

Kaela of the Vale. Kael of Sol'Ryn. Dorne the Ashmarked. Kaelaria Flame-Born.

She reached out with trembling hands and opened the cover.

The handwriting was hers.

Her breath caught.

The first page was dated over four hundred years ago.

Cycle 1:

Met him beneath the third moon. He was afraid. I was cruel. I kissed him before he spoke my name.

Cycle 2:

He tried to kill me before I remembered. I think I loved him anyway.

Cycle 6:

We made it to the river. I almost believed it would last. It didn't.

Cycle 12:

He begged me to forget. I couldn't. So I made us both forget.

Kaela flipped through the pages, each one denser, the ink darker, as if even memory began to burn the longer it endured.

Images rose unbidden.

A battlefield at dusk.

A hidden temple in the ice.

A marketplace where he handed her fruit with shaking hands.

A prison cell. A knife.

A kiss. A goodbye.

A vow, always, *always,* repeated in a language she could never read until it was too late.

She reached the middle.

Cycle 49:

He betrayed me.

The words were a scar. Carved, not written.

Cycle 50:

I forgave him.

Cycle 51:

I betrayed him.

Kaela turned the page with fingers that shook.

Some entries were no more than single lines. Others were full pages of frantic, aching scrawl.

Cycle 67:

We grew old together. He died before me. I forgot what his voice sounded like.

Cycle 72:

He remembered first. He tried to make me see. I killed him before I could.

Kaela froze.

Ezren stepped closer behind her.

"Kaela?" he whispered.

She turned the final page.

Her own handwriting stared back at her.

But it had been written *recently*.

The ink was still wet.

Cycle 100:

You must remember him before you kill him again.

Kaela couldn't breathe.

Ezren moved beside her, reading over her shoulder. His expression didn't change—but the lines around his eyes deepened.

He had known.

Part of him had always known.

"I've killed you," Kaela whispered. "Again and again."

He didn't speak.

Tears blurred her vision. She clutched the book to her chest, staggered away from the pedestal, from the truth of her own hand. "Why didn't you tell me?"

"Because I never remembered *before* you," he said quietly. "Not completely. Not in time."

She shook her head, heart pounding. "But the last page—someone wrote it—*I* wrote it—"

"You wrote it in the last life," he said. "Before the curse reset."

She looked at him, stunned.

Ezren met her eyes.

"I don't know how we broke through this time. Maybe the eclipse. Maybe the unraveling."

"Maybe because we *chose* to," she whispered.

He stepped closer. "I remember the tower. The vow. The kiss under the falling stars."

"So do I," she said. "But why does it still hurt? Why does every time we touch feel like a blade?"

Ezren didn't answer.

Because the answer was already blooming between them—bitter, terrible, beautiful.

Love had never been the curse.

The vow had never been punishment.

They had done this to themselves.

To protect something.

Or to hide something.

Kaela turned to the back of the book. There were no more entries.

But a single rune was drawn in the center of the inside cover.

She didn't recognize it.

But her bones did.

"It's the root glyph," Ezren said. "The first syllable of the soul-vow. The part we've never spoken aloud."

Kaela reached toward it—

And the room screamed.

Light erupted from the book, slamming into her chest.

Ezren grabbed her—

And the loop began again.

A mountain peak.

A battlefield.

A kiss.

A betrayal.
A blade in her hand.
His voice, crying her name.
A spell.
A scream.
A silence.
And then—
She was back.
In the Vault.
Book in her hands.
Ezren on the floor beside her, unconscious.
Kaela stood in the middle of the memory storm.
And realized:
The curse hadn't been broken.
It had simply evolved.
And the only way out—
Was through the very thing they feared most.
Each other.

The Vault pulsed around her—walls vibrating like lungs drawing breath, floor humming with latent magic stirred from slumber. Kaela stood rooted in the heart of it all, the diary clutched in bloodless fingers, her mind fractured with memories that were and were not her own.

Ezren lay on the floor, unmoving but alive, his chest rising and falling in shallow gasps.

Kaela's pulse thundered in her ears, drowning out the silence. Her knees buckled, and she dropped beside him, cradling his head, her voice barely a whisper.

"Ezren… please."

His eyes fluttered open.

The Spells We Wove with Forgotten Words

But they weren't right.

Not yet.

They flickered with lifetimes—eyes too full of knowing, of pain, of *endings.*

Kaela pressed her forehead to his.

And then it hit her.

They were still in the loop.

The spell, the vow, the memories—they weren't just haunting them.

They were *programming* them.

Built like runes in a circle, designed to repeat. Each cycle a reset. Each death a rebirth. Each life another tragic attempt at breaking free.

Kaela clenched her jaw.

They were the sigils in the center of a spell they'd cast too well.

And if they didn't finish it properly, it would *never stop.*

She looked back at the book.

The rune on the last page shimmered faintly, as though daring her to try again.

Ezren stirred in her arms. "Kaela…"

"I'm here," she said, wiping soot from his face.

He focused on her slowly. "I saw it. The first loop."

"So did I."

His voice cracked. "We made ourselves forget."

"We made ourselves *kill.*"

He shuddered. "We tried to bind love with blood. We made a vow not to *stay together*—but to *never stop searching,* even if it killed us."

"And it always did," Kaela whispered.

Ezren sat up, wincing. His fingers brushed hers. She didn't

pull away.

This time, the pain didn't come.

Just warmth.

Just silence.

Different.

The curse was *shifting*.

Kaela opened the book again and stared at the glyph.

"This is the root," she said. "The seed we buried in ourselves."

"It's the key," Ezren replied. "But it won't open the door unless we both speak it."

Together, they placed their palms on the page.

The glyph pulsed—then *burned*.

Not with fire.

With *memory*.

Suddenly, the vault fell away.

They were falling.

No ground. No sky. Only time, spiraling around them in threads of light and sound. Every version of themselves, spinning like torn pages from a forgotten epic.

A hundred Kaelas. A hundred Ezrens.

One stabbed him.

One abandoned her.

One died in childbirth.

One cursed him.

One forgave.

One never found him at all.

Then—

They landed.

A stone circle on a rainy hilltop.

Not memory.

Not illusion.

The Spells We Wove with Forgotten Words

Origin.

Kaela gasped as wind ripped through her cloak. She looked down—and saw her own hands, younger, calloused, holding a blood-soaked blade. Ezren stood across from her, his shirt torn, rain pouring down his face, his hands shaking.

This was *before* the vow.

Before the Binding.

Before the kiss.

This was the moment they made the choice.

Kaela fell to her knees.

Ezren mirrored her, breath catching.

The air was electric with potential. With *danger.*

They weren't being *shown* the memory.

They were *inside* it.

And this time, they had the power to change it.

Kaela raised her eyes to him. "We don't have to do it."

Ezren's voice trembled. "You said you would die without me."

"I will."

"But if we cast it again…"

"We'll loop forever."

He reached for her face, cupped it gently, reverently.

"I'd rather forget you a thousand times than lose you once."

Her tears mingled with rain. "And I'd rather *remember* the end than keep reliving the beginning."

Their foreheads touched.

Lightning split the sky.

And together, they spoke—not in the soul-language, but in their *own.*

The spell they never dared speak before.

"We release each other."

"We remember by choice, not curse."
"We forgive what the loop taught us to fear."
"We live. We *end*."

The world ruptured around them.

The hill exploded in light—every fragment of every cycle combusting into ash.

Kaela screamed—

Ezren's arms around her—

And the loop shattered.

She woke to birdsong.

Real birds.

Sunlight filtered through the broken ceiling of the Vault. Dust motes danced lazily in the golden air.

Kaela blinked up at the sky.

The book was gone.

Ezren sat beside her, breathing evenly, his face relaxed for the first time in all the lives she could remember.

He opened his eyes.

Smiled.

"Did we do it?" he asked.

Kaela leaned into him, resting her head on his shoulder.

"I think we did."

There was no ache in her chest.

No searing memory.

Only the now.

And for the first time in a hundred lives—

That was enough.

Eleven

The Betrayer's Mark

The moon hung low, swollen and honey-colored over the jagged rim of the Western Wastes. The night air hummed with unseen things—arcane residue, the tension of spells unraveling, the memory of wars long settled into the dust. Kaela and Ezren made camp in a hollow beneath a spine of obsidian rock, far from any road and deliberately distant from the whispering ruins of Caladris.

They hadn't spoken much since they left the vault.

Not because of silence.

But because the silence was *safe*.

Ezren sat just outside the flickering reach of their campfire, his back to the crag wall, shirt discarded, fingers shaking slightly as they skimmed over the symbol branded into his skin.

It pulsed beneath his ribs—ugly, old, and alive.

A broken ring wrapped in thorns.

The Betrayer's Mark

The Mark of the Betrayer.

He hadn't seen it until this morning.

It hadn't been there before.

Not in this life.

Not in this *body*.

But when he'd caught his reflection in the pool outside the vault—saw the distorted twist of runes crawling over his ribs—he knew. It wasn't a scar. It wasn't a wound.

It was a *curse*.

Cast by Kaela.

Not *this* Kaela.

But one of her past selves.

And now it was awake.

His jaw tightened as he pressed his palm over it. It felt hot beneath the skin—searing if Kaela came too close, as if it *remembered* her before he did.

He couldn't tell her.

Not yet.

Not after everything they'd just survived. Not after the vow had been broken, the Binding unmade, and their memories had begun to mend in ways that felt like breathing again instead of drowning.

But the mark whispered.

Low. Always.

She will do it again.

She remembers the kiss. But not the knife.

She *always* chooses the knife.

Ezren closed his eyes. Breathed.

Tried to ignore it.

Behind him, Kaela slept—curled on one side, her hand tucked beneath her cheek. Her hair spilled across the ground like ink, catching the firelight in copper threads. She looked peaceful. Vulnerable in a way she never showed awake.

He wondered if she would ever forgive him.

Not just for the secrets.

But for *deserving* the curse.

Because in the echo of memory, somewhere behind the noise and pain and magic, he *remembered*.

A tower.

A lie.

A stolen artifact.

A betrayal.

His.

He remembered her scream. The look in her eyes before she whispered the curse. The way her voice didn't shake—not because she wasn't afraid, but because she loved him too much to allow hesitation.

And then—

Centuries.

Lifetimes.

A hundred Kaelas, all of them carrying the echo of that moment, even if they didn't know why.

The loop had broken, but the fragments remained. And now this one—this Kaela—trusted him.

He wasn't sure he'd earned it.

He wasn't sure he *could*.

The next morning, they moved fast.

The land south of Caladris was shifting—rivers changing course, roads collapsing into fissures where old magic boiled beneath the crust. Every now and then, they passed travelers who'd lost more than direction. People with blank eyes and scarred memories. People who whispered Kaela's name with

The Betrayer's Mark

awe or fear or both.

The Binding hadn't just stitched time.

It had *rewritten* history.

Ezren kept his distance during the day, always walking just behind her, his hand rarely brushing hers. When she reached for him, he found excuses—adjusting his satchel, scouting ahead, shifting the campfire.

Kaela noticed.

Of course she did.

On the fourth night, she finally spoke.

"You're hiding something," she said, voice low, firelight dancing in her eyes.

Ezren paused mid-motion, half-draped in his cloak.

He forced a casual shrug. "Aren't we both?"

She didn't smile.

"You flinch when I touch you."

"Don't be ridiculous."

"Ezren."

His name, spoken softly, but with weight.

He sighed, rubbing a hand through his hair. "I'm... tired. That's all."

Kaela stared at him. She didn't blink.

And for a moment, he thought she might drop it.

But then she crossed the space between them.

And touched his chest.

Her fingers stopped an inch above the mark, right where the skin had begun to discolor again.

Ezren tensed.

Kaela's eyes widened.

She pulled his shirt open without warning, the fabric slipping over his shoulder—and froze.

The sigil stared back at her.

Black and angry, coiled like a snake with no end.

Her voice dropped to a whisper. "What is that?"

He tried to step back.

She grabbed his wrist.

"*Ezren.* What is it?"

He swallowed.

Then gave up the lie.

"It's a curse."

"From who?"

He met her eyes.

The silence said it all.

Her breath caught.

Her hand dropped.

She stepped back like he'd struck her.

"No," she whispered. "I would never—"

"You did."

"*Not me.*"

Ezren nodded. "Another you."

Kaela shook her head, as if she could physically throw the memory off. "I don't remember doing that."

"You wouldn't. She buried it deep. But the curse knew when the Binding ended. It came back."

"But why?" she whispered. "What did you do to her?"

Ezren looked away.

And that was the answer.

Kaela stared at him. "You betrayed me."

He didn't argue.

The fire snapped between them.

Kaela's voice trembled. "Tell me. Tell me what you did."

Ezren closed his eyes. "I stole the anchor."

"What anchor?"

"The original artifact. The one we built the first loop around. I took it. Sold it. I—" He laughed bitterly. "I told myself I was saving us. That I was breaking the cycle. But I just... broke you."

Her silence was worse than shouting.

"I should've told you sooner," he said. "I was afraid."

"Of me?" she asked.

"No. Of the *truth*. That I'm not who you remember. That maybe I never was."

Kaela turned her back to him.

The wind picked up, scattering ash from the fire.

Then—

"I'm not her either," she said.

He looked at her.

She didn't turn around.

"I've done things. In other lives. In this one. I've killed. Lied. Run." She paused. "But I never cursed you out of hate."

Ezren's throat worked. "I know."

"You should've told me."

"I wanted to be the man you thought I was."

"I never asked you to be perfect," she said. "I just asked you to be *honest*."

Silence.

Long and cold.

She walked away from the fire, past the edge of the clearing, into the dark. Not far.

But far enough.

Ezren sat alone, the mark burning on his chest.

And for the first time in all his lives—

He wasn't sure if love was enough.

The Spells We Wove with Forgotten Words

The night stretched on.

Above, the stars blinked behind a drifting veil of smoke, as if the sky, too, was uncertain of its shape. Kaela sat on a fallen tree just beyond the reach of the firelight, fingers curled into fists in her lap, staring into the blackness of the woods ahead.

She was cold.

But she didn't go back to the fire.

She didn't want warmth from someone who couldn't give her the truth.

Her heartbeat was a drumbeat behind her eyes. The sigil on Ezren's chest had burned into her memory like a second moon — not because of what it was, but because *she* had put it there.

A Kaela not her, yet *still her.*

A truth buried beneath centuries of grief.

What else am I capable of?

She'd thought she was past the worst of it. The vow broken. The loop undone. Her memories her own again. But then came *this,* the proof that even in freedom, the past could slither into the present and choke the breath from her trust.

A twig cracked behind her.

Kaela didn't turn.

"I need to know," she said flatly. "Is it still active?"

Ezren stopped just short of her.

His voice was hoarse. "I don't know."

She turned, slowly. "Then you've felt it, haven't you? That flare in your ribs when I get too close. That *pulse.* You think I haven't noticed?"

Ezren's shoulders dropped. "I wasn't trying to lie."

"You were hiding."

"I didn't want to *make* you remember."

Kaela stood, her voice low and dangerous now. "You think

you *protect* me by hiding pieces of yourself? That trust is something you *safeguard* by silence?"

"No," he said. "I think trust is something you *lose* forever the moment you say something that sounds like a mistake instead of the truth."

They stared at each other.

The woods around them quieted.

Then Kaela stepped forward—close enough that the curse beneath his skin began to throb. She could feel it now, as if her magic recognized its own echo. A tether, sharp and hot, tying them together in a knot neither of them had meant to tie.

"I remember something else," she said softly. "Not the moment I cast the mark… but what I felt before I did."

Ezren swallowed. "What did you feel?"

She lifted a hand, fingertips hovering above his chest—right where the mark lay under skin and blood and guilt.

"Betrayal," she whispered. "Not just rage. Not revenge. It was heartbreak twisted into spellcraft. It wasn't just about what you *did*. It was about what you *meant*. You made me doubt the one thing I was willing to burn the world for."

Ezren said nothing.

Kaela lowered her hand, stepped back.

"I don't hate you," she said.

"But you don't trust me."

"Not yet."

He took a breath. "Then let me prove it."

She looked at him, wary.

Ezren reached into his satchel and withdrew a small obsidian mirror, its surface rippling with distortion.

"I found this at the edge of the vault," he said. "It holds reflections—*honest* ones. If we bind our names to it, it will reveal *everything*. No illusions. No half-truths."

Kaela's eyes narrowed. "Even from past lives?"

Ezren nodded. "Especially from past lives."

"You're willing to show me?"

"I'm willing to bleed," he said.

Her throat tightened.

Kaela stepped forward. Together, they placed a drop of blood each onto the mirror's edge. The stone flared, shimmering with light. Images began to ripple across the surface—flashes of lives before, flickering too fast to hold.

But one moment surfaced and held.

Ezren.

Standing at the foot of a tower, the stolen artifact in hand. His face twisted in conflict. Behind him, a Kaela in white armor climbing the stairs, calling his name.

Another image:

Kaela weeping beside his dying body, whispering the words of the curse—not in fury.

But in *grief*.

Then another:

Ezren binding the first fire-loop without her knowledge, convinced he was saving them.

Then:

Kaela erasing her memory, certain she would kill him again if she didn't.

They stood in silence as the mirror flickered out.

Truth. Whole. Undeniable.

Ezren let out a long, unsteady breath. "Now you know."

Kaela didn't speak. She didn't move.

He waited.

And then—

The Betrayer's Mark

She stepped forward.

Not to strike.

Not to run.

But to press her forehead to his, gently.

"I won't promise to forget," she said. "But I'll try to forgive."

Ezren closed his eyes. "That's enough."

They stood like that, tethered not by curse or loop or vow—but by a new kind of magic.

One made not of spells.

But of choice.

Still bruised.

Still burning.

But *theirs*.

Behind them, the fire crackled.

Ahead of them, the road twisted deeper into the unknown.

And for the first time, they walked it side by side.

Twelve

The Hollow Moon Rises

Night came early to the Vale of Oren.

The land itself seemed to sense what approached—an ancient stillness settling over the broken stones, the wind dying mid-breath, the clouds retreating into the distance as if unwilling to witness what the sky would birth.

Kaela stood at the edge of the glade, her eyes fixed on the low eastern horizon. The magical moon—the *Hollow Moon*, as it was named in forgotten texts—hung fat and trembling just beneath the line of trees. Pale silver streaks lined its rim, and its surface pulsed faintly like a waiting heartbeat. It wasn't due to rise for another hour, but its presence was already warping the air, causing shimmer-lines to ripple across the ground like heatwaves.

Ezren came up beside her, slow and wary, his footsteps careful through the brittle grass.

The Hollow Moon Rises

"We shouldn't be this close," he said. "This valley was one of the leyline convergence sites during the first cycle."

Kaela didn't turn her head. "I know."

"You think it'll anchor us?"

"I think it will test us."

They didn't speak again.

Not for a long time.

Behind them, their campsite lay in unnatural silence. No night-birds. No whispering trees. Just the slow thrum of the Hollow Moon's pull—growing heavier with every second.

And then, without warning—

The moon *rose.*

Not like the real moon, slow and stately.

No.

This one *jerked* upward—dragged as if by invisible chains—and shone with an inner light that wasn't reflected sunlight but something *deeper*. Older. Light that didn't illuminate, but peeled.

Kaela gasped.

Ezren staggered back a step.

The world around them *shivered.*

And cracked.

Kaela blinked—

And the glade was gone.

She stood in a throne room.

She knew this place.

Velanthis, seat of the Starborne Queens. Marble pillars twisted with gold-veined ivy. A vault of glass overhead where stars shimmered like breath frozen in crystal.

She wore white. Gloves. A coronet. Her hands were bloodless on the hilt of a ceremonial blade.

Ezren knelt at her feet.

Chains around his wrists.

The throne behind her was empty.

No ruler but her.

This had happened.

A past life.

Cycle... *thirty-one*?

She stepped down before she thought, watching herself—*her other self*—move with calculated precision. This Kaela did not tremble. This Kaela was ice.

"Ezren of the Hollow Flame," she said, voice clipped and cold. "You are accused of high treason, oathbreaking, and memory manipulation."

He looked up, defiant and beautiful and broken all at once.

"I did it for you," he said.

"You did it for power."

"I *remembered* you before you remembered me," he snarled. "And I paid the price. Again and again. You cursed me, Kaela. You made me *suffer* for daring to *love* you."

The other Kaela's hands didn't move.

But her eyes glistened.

Ezren's head bowed.

She watched her own lips whisper the sentence.

"Execute him."

The memory *shattered*.

Kaela jerked upright—heart pounding, palms slick, breath short.

She was back in the glade.

The Hollow Moon had risen fully now. It hung massive above them, flooding the clearing with silver so bright it bled the color from everything else.

"Ezren?" she called.

No answer.

She turned—

And he was gone.

Ezren woke in a tower of obsidian.

Chains.

Again.

But this time, the chains were fire. Not metaphor. Not magic. Real flame, licking at his wrists but refusing to consume him.

He turned his head—

And saw her.

Kaela.

Or *a* Kaela.

This one wore red. Her face was wild with grief and fury, her hair loose, her eyes ringed with sleepless shadows. She stood before him, sword in one hand, a ring in the other.

"I gave you everything," she said. "And you sold it for *a book*."

Ezren's mouth was dry.

He remembered this.

Cycle forty-four.

He'd been desperate. The world had been collapsing. The spell was fading. He thought he could stabilize the anchor by selling it to the Lore Merchants—buying them time.

She thought he betrayed her.

She'd branded him with the sigil.

Right *here.*

The Kaela in front of him stepped closer, the ring glinting in her hand.

"Say you don't love me," she whispered. "Just *say it,* and I'll make it painless."

He looked her in the eye.

The Spells We Wove with Forgotten Words

And said nothing.

Because he *did* love her.

Even then.

She screamed.

And placed the ring against his chest.

Pain exploded through him as fire etched the Betrayer's Mark into his flesh.

Ezren crumpled—

And woke in the glade, screaming.

Kaela was already at his side, clutching his shoulders.

"It's the moon," she said, breathless. "It's *trapping us* in the cycles. Forcing us to relive the worst moments."

He clutched at her wrist, his body still convulsing with phantom pain. "We're bleeding memories."

"What?"

Ezren sat upright, gasping. "Every time we fall into a past life, we're leaking. *Losing parts* of who we are. I couldn't remember your face when I woke up. Not this one."

Kaela's face blanched. "We have to anchor. *Now.* Before it pulls us under completely."

She stood, drew her dagger, and sliced her palm without hesitation.

Blood hit the ground.

The leyline beneath the glade flared to life.

Ezren followed suit, biting down as the blade cut deep.

Their blood met on the stone.

Magic roared.

The Hollow Moon *screamed.*

The air warped—ripping open again—

And this time, Kaela found herself at sea.

The deck of a burning ship.

Ezren dying in her arms.

Her own sword in his gut.

"Why?" he gasped.

She couldn't speak.

Because she didn't know.

Not in that life.

Not in this one.

Ezren woke again in a dark corridor, watching Kaela vanish into fire.

Then in a castle.

Then in a prison.

Over and over.

Until he didn't know which version of him was *real*.

Until he didn't *want* to wake up.

But one memory grounded him.

Always.

The *first kiss*.

Under starlight.

Kaela's lips cold from the wind.

Her hands trembling as she touched his cheek.

"Even if we forget," she whispered, "don't forget *this*."

That kiss exploded into light—

And Ezren surged upright.

Kaela was there, gasping, mirroring him.

Their eyes locked.

This time, they *remembered*.

They reached for each other—

Their fingers laced—

And the Hollow Moon *broke*.

Not with sound.

But with silence.

It cracked like glass and dissolved into stardust, pouring across the glade in a wave of soft silver.

The ground settled.

The sky cleared.

And Kaela collapsed into his arms.

They were soaked in sweat. Shaking. Bruised by memory.

But they were here.

Now.

Together.

And for the first time since the spell began, they *chose* to hold on.

The glade was silent now, save for the rasp of breath and the whispering hush of leaves resettling themselves after a long tremor. The ground beneath Kaela and Ezren still radiated faint warmth, as if the leyline buried deep below hadn't quite finished pulsing.

Kaela lay with her head against Ezren's chest, his heartbeat thudding in a slow, stuttered rhythm beneath her ear. Every bone in her body ached, but she didn't move. Neither did he.

Their blood—mingled where it had struck the circle of stone—glowed faintly between them, the anchor they'd made holding fast, like a line thrown across a rising sea.

They had survived the Hollow Moon.

But barely.

Ezren stirred beneath her, arms curling tighter.

"I saw the first loop again," he whispered. "But it was different this time."

Kaela lifted her head, watching the strange sheen of his eyes in the fading starlight. "What changed?"

"You didn't run."

Her breath caught.

"You always ran in the end," he said. "Every time. Right before it looped. You always chose duty or magic or—" he swallowed, "—anything but me."

Kaela was quiet for a long moment.

Then, softly, "I think I always thought love couldn't survive the fire. That it had to be something you protect from magic, not *through* it."

Ezren's thumb brushed the edge of her jaw. "It can survive anything. Except silence."

They lay there in the middle of the broken glade, surrounded by shattered time, and Kaela felt something inside her shift. Not a memory. Not a spell.

Something deeper.

Resolve.

She sat up slowly, glancing around them.

Everything the moon had touched was scorched. The glade was rimmed with blackened stone, trees hollowed out from the inside. The air tasted of ash and silver.

"We're not done," she said, voice steady.

Ezren nodded. "No. But the Hollow Moon is. The worst of its pull has passed."

She stood carefully, testing her limbs. "It's not just about surviving now. It's about *sealing*. We left too many threads dangling. Too many memories half-closed. The loop is broken, but the spell is frayed across the world. The Hollow Moon just proved it—it's still *bleeding*."

Ezren rose beside her, his face solemn. "Then we finish what we started."

Kaela walked to the edge of the circle, where their blood had carved its way into the cracks between stones. She bent and pressed her fingers to it. The glow was fading, but the signature remained.

It had worked.

But it wouldn't last.

"Ezren," she said slowly. "Do you remember the second glyph?"

He blinked. "The one from the Vault?"

"No. Earlier. In the Binding design—hidden behind the memory-spell. The one that *folded time,* not just protected it."

He frowned, thinking, then cursed softly. "Yes. It was under the name sigils. Fused into the spell's skeleton."

Kaela turned to him. "I think that's what's still active."

Ezren looked toward the sky, where the Hollow Moon had vanished. "The fold."

She nodded. "We didn't just bind ourselves to each other. We folded ourselves *into* the world. Over and over. That's why the past lives kept looping. Why the Hollow Moon pulled us through them."

Ezren's expression darkened. "And if the fold's still open—"

"It's only a matter of time before it happens again."

They stared at each other.

Kaela took a slow, shaky breath. "We have to go back to where we cast the fold."

Ezren flinched. "Kael. That place—"

"I know."

"It killed us."

"I know."

He hesitated. "You think it's still there?"

"If the glyph remains, yes. It was carved into the spine of the world itself. We used the rootstone as a focus. That magic doesn't decay."

Ezren nodded grimly. "Then we need to reach the Vale of

Thorns."

Kaela swallowed hard.

The Vale of Thorns was the place they never spoke of. Not even in memory.

It was where the first failure happened.

The first death.

The first forgetting.

Kaela turned toward the horizon, where dawn was beginning to bleed gold across the ashes.

"We'll go," she said. "And we'll end it."

Ezren stepped beside her, his arm brushing hers. He didn't touch her fully—still cautious, still careful. But his presence was enough. Warm. Steady.

For the first time in hundreds of years, they walked not into love.

But *through* it.

Side by side.

Unlooped.

And unafraid.

Thirteen

The Archive of Echoes

The entrance was a whisper in the stone.

Kaela almost missed it—tucked beneath a shattered ridge of quartz, the opening no larger than a coffin's lid and sealed in a shimmer of air that felt like breath. The wind died as she approached, as if the world itself was holding still. Her boots crunched over crystal dust. Her palm, cut days ago and barely healed, began to ache again.

Ezren waited behind her, his presence steady as always—but she could feel the way he watched her. Not urging. Not pushing. Just *waiting*.

Only *she* could enter.

Only *she* could ask.

Kaela knelt and pressed her hand to the shimmer.

It recoiled at first, a ripple across the air like ink dropped in water.

Then it accepted her.

The Archive of Echoes

The shimmer vanished.

Stone parted like skin under a scalpel.

The entrance yawned wide, darkness spilling out like old secrets.

Ezren stepped forward. "Are you sure—"

"I have to," she said. "We can't close the fold without the original incantation. And it's in there. The Archive hears all."

He nodded. "Just… come back."

She looked at him—eyes full of more memories than anyone should carry—and stepped into the dark.

The entrance sealed behind her.

Total silence.

And then—

Music.

Faint. Strange. Like wind chimes echoing underwater.

The passage ahead glowed not with light, but memory. Threads of golden mist floated in the air like drifting thoughts. They hummed as she passed through them, each one brushing against her mind with flashes of *things she had never seen*.

A child in a tower, whispering spells into a storm.

An old woman in a field, drawing runes in the dirt with her blood.

A prince screaming a curse as his kingdom fell.

Every spell ever spoken.

Every word ever woven with intent.

They lived here, in the Archive of Echoes.

The walls were lined with veins of polished crystal, each one pulsing faintly. Runes flickered across the stone like fireflies, drifting and reassembling constantly—living syntax.

Kaela's heart pounded.

The air tasted like magic too old for names.

And then, ahead of her, a figure appeared—tall, shrouded in robes of starlight and shadow, faceless but *watching*.

The Archivist.

"Kaela Dorne," it said, its voice like bells rung through water. "You come seeking the Folded Tongue. The spell that wrote you into the marrow of the world."

She nodded once. "Yes."

The Archivist tilted its head. "To speak it whole, you must *remember* him wholly. Ezren Valen. Not as lover. Not as memory. But as *truth*. Every life. Every betrayal. Every breath."

"I'm ready," Kaela said.

"No," the Archivist replied. "You are not."

She stiffened.

"To remember fully," it said, "you must forget. A piece of you must be given in exchange."

Kaela's breath hitched.

"What do you mean?"

"Your memory is full. Woven tight as thread on a loom. To make space for the whole of him, *something must be unmade.*"

The Archivist raised a hand.

A shimmer of mist formed in the air.

Three faces bloomed into view.

Kaela's sister—Sera, her laughter bright and wild, always windburned from flying over cliff roads on her alchemist glider.

Her father—Alric Dorne, long dead, but ever-etched into her bones with the smell of leather and old books, the man who taught her to read spells *like poetry*.

And her mentor—Eryndel, the one who had pulled her from ruin, who had taught her how to fight, how to *survive*, how to stay *human* even when the world tried to turn her into something else.

The Archivist's voice was soft. "Choose one. And you will forget them. Not just now. *Forever.*"

Kaela staggered back. "No."

The Archivist didn't move.

"I can't. That's not a choice. That's a *butchery.*"

"You want to close the fold," it said. "You want to stop the world from unraveling. You want to *save* him."

"I shouldn't have to trade one for the other."

"All memory is spellwork," the Archivist said. "And every spell has its cost."

The air grew colder.

The images sharpened.

Sera—laughing in the rain, hair sticking to her cheeks, pulling Kaela into the downpour without care.

Alric—reading aloud beside a fire, his hand on her shoulder, a book of ancient star-rituals in his lap.

Eryndel—bleeding from the ribs, sword in hand, whispering *"Run, Kael. You're not ready to die yet."*

Kaela fell to her knees.

Her voice cracked. "Why me?"

"Because you wrote the vow," the Archivist said. "Because you made the loop. Because you folded time around love and called it destiny."

Kaela clenched her fists.

Tears welled in her eyes.

Then—

She stood.

And looked at each image.

She stepped toward the one of her father.

Paused.

The Spells We Wove with Forgotten Words

Then to Sera.
Paused.
Then Eryndel.
And stopped.
Her heart broke as she whispered, "I'm sorry."
The mist rippled.
Eryndel's face began to fade.
"Wait—" Kaela gasped, stepping back. "No, I—"
But the Archivist raised a hand.
"It is done."
Kaela choked on a sob.
And then—something *broke.*
She felt it tear out of her like a root yanked from stone.
The memory of Eryndel.
Gone.
His name.
Gone.
She stumbled back, clutching her head.
"Who was I choosing?" she whispered.
The Archivist didn't answer.
But a door opened behind it—tall and golden and glowing with runes that *knew her.*
"Go," the Archivist said.
Kaela walked through the door with steps that trembled.
On the other side:
A circle of flame.
Floating in the air, held in stasis, was a string of glyphs—long, winding, *impossibly old.* They pulsed in time with her heartbeat. Her blood sang in response.
The Folded Tongue.
The original incantation.

She reached out—
And the spell *entered* her.
Not just as words.
But as *understanding.*
She saw Ezren.
In every life.
Not just in love, but in *loss.*
She saw the betrayal.
She saw her knife in his back.
She saw his hands building the spell that broke them.
She saw the vow, carved from desperation and hope and fear.
And she saw *him*—raw, human, flawed, *real.*
The spell settled in her bones.
Kaela dropped to her knees.
And whispered, "I remember you now."
The Archive pulsed around her.
And the door reopened.
Ezren stood on the other side.
Eyes wide.
"You're bleeding," he said, rushing to her.
She looked at him—really looked at him—and wept.
"I had to forget someone," she whispered.
His arms closed around her.
"I'm sorry," he said. "I'm so sorry."
"No," she said. "Not this time."
Because now, she *knew* him.
And now, they could finally *end it.*

Ezren held her as though she were vanishing in his arms.
Kaela's head rested against his shoulder, her body limp with

exhaustion, yet still tense with something deeper than fatigue. Not pain. Not grief. But *absence*.

There was a hole inside her now.

And though she couldn't name it, her magic could feel the shape of it—like a wound she couldn't see, but could feel bleed.

Ezren's voice was low in her ear. "Who did you lose?"

Kaela pulled back slowly. Her eyes searched his, the words forming at the edge of her mouth—

Then dissolving.

"I… I don't know."

Ezren stilled.

Her brow furrowed. "I know I made a choice. I can feel the scar it left. But I don't remember the name. Or their face. Just… weight."

Ezren's gaze darkened. "The Archive made you choose."

She nodded. "It was the price. To make space for all of you—all the yous—I had to lose something else."

His jaw tightened. "That's not a fair trade."

"There's no fairness in magic," she said, her voice thin but steady. "Only cost."

He helped her to her feet, keeping one arm wrapped around her waist. "Can you stand?"

"Standing isn't the problem," she murmured. "Walking away is."

Together, they left the Archive.

The stone shimmered closed behind them, the entrance folding back into the mountain like a mouth swallowing its last word. As they stepped out beneath the dusk-streaked sky, the Hollow Moon now long gone, Kaela sucked in a breath of the cold, real air.

It tasted wrong.

The Archive of Echoes

Like a note missing from a melody.

Ezren didn't speak as they returned to the path, the mountains stretching behind them like jagged memories.

But Kaela was thinking.

Not just about who she lost.

But what she'd *gained*.

The Folded Tongue burned faintly beneath her skin, woven through her blood now, humming to her bones. She could feel the power of the original incantation whispering beneath every heartbeat—*not just the spell to end the loop, but the truth of it.*

They hadn't merely woven a time-bind between two lovers.

They had laced their identities into the ley-thread of the world.

The spell hadn't protected their love.

It had *enslaved* it.

Not to each other.

But to the concept of always.

It was never meant to be a sanctuary.

It was a *trap*.

"Kaela," Ezren said quietly, his voice cutting through the silence like a knife. "We have a problem."

She turned, the wind brushing strands of hair against her cheek.

He was holding something.

A letter.

The paper aged and ink-faded. Tucked beneath a crystal near the campfire where he'd been waiting outside the Archive.

He handed it to her.

Kaela unfolded it, the handwriting jagged and barely legible—but she recognized it.

Her own.
But it wasn't recent.
It was older. Much older.
From a life she couldn't name.
She read:

> If you're reading this, then I made it far enough to reach the Archive.
> And if you made it further, then you know what it costs.
> This is your last chance, Kaela. Do not close the loop.
> Do not seal the fold.
> End it, yes. But do not bind it shut.
> Because if you do, he dies.
> Not again.
> Forever.

Kaela's hand trembled.
Ezren said nothing.
She read the last line:

> You cannot carry him through the spell and leave the door open. You must choose. Memory or man. Magic or love. You cannot have both.

Kaela crushed the letter in her fist, heart thundering in her chest.
"No," she whispered. "No—this can't be another choice."
Ezren knelt beside her. "What does it mean?"
She opened her hand, staring down at the ruined paper.

"It means," she said hollowly, "if I seal the fold, it will consume everything that ever *was* you. The spell will collapse. You'll be set free."

"That sounds like what we want."

"No," Kaela said. "Not *set free* like life. Set free like... *erased.*"

Ezren was quiet.

She looked at him, eyes wild. "You'll die, Ezren. Not just now. Everywhere. All of you. Every version I just remembered—every kiss, every mistake, every moment—we'll have *nothing*. Not even memory."

His hand touched hers.

Gently.

"Then don't seal it," he said.

Kaela's voice broke. "But the world—"

"We've saved the world before," he whispered. "We've *burned* for it. Died for it. Forgotten each other for it."

"I can't lose you," she said.

"And I can't ask you to let the world tear itself apart."

She looked away, shaking.

Ezren cupped her face, pulled her eyes back to his.

"If this is my end," he said, "then let me choose it."

She shook her head. "There has to be another way."

"There isn't. There never was. We built this like a trap, Kaela. The key to close it is *us*. One of us has to go."

Kaela turned her face into his hand, tears streaking her cheeks. "Then I choose me."

Ezren stilled.

"I choose to go," she whispered. "You live. You *stay.*"

"No—"

She pulled back. "Don't argue. You've died a hundred times for me. Let me carry you this time."

The Spells We Wove with Forgotten Words

"Kaela—"

She drew the Folded Tongue into her palm, the sigil forming in fire and blood.

Ezren grabbed her wrist. "You don't have to—"

"I already lost someone today," she whispered. "I'm not losing *you*."

And then—

She spoke the incantation.

The final form of the Folded Tongue.

The spell flared into the air around them, wind shrieking through the trees, the sky cracking with light. Symbols burned in the earth, twisting through every name they'd ever borne, every path they'd ever taken.

Ezren screamed her name.

Kaela looked at him.

Smiled.

"Remember me," she said.

And stepped into the center of the spell.

Light consumed her.

Ezren lunged.

But it was too late.

She was gone.

The fold collapsed inward—

And then, silence.

Utter, perfect silence.

Ezren fell to his knees, hands empty.

Around him, the world was still.

The loop was broken.

The spell sealed.

And Kaela Dorne—

Was gone.

Fourteen

Fire Between Us

The cell was small. Stone walls pressed in from every side, slick with condensation, veins of silence-weaving runes pulsing faintly beneath the surface. The floor sloped downward toward a grate that stank of old blood and sanctified ash.

Ezren lay crumpled on the floor, shackled by wrists and ankles, his magic stripped from him by a circle of twisted sigils carved directly into his skin.

He had stopped screaming hours ago.

Now he simply breathed.

In.

Out.

Each inhale scraped through his chest like broken glass, shallow and wet.

He didn't know how long he'd been here.

The Order of the Silenced did not measure time in ways that

mattered to men.

They measured it in truths.

And pain.

Bootsteps echoed through the corridor beyond his cell—soft, almost reverent.

He didn't lift his head. Not at first.

He *knew* the rhythm.

Not military.

Liturgical.

They weren't guards.

They were priests.

One of them stepped into the light—a woman clad in grey, robes fluttering like smoke around her.

Her face was covered by a silver mask, expressionless and cold, except for the narrow slits where eyes gleamed beneath.

She knelt beside him.

"Ezren Valen," she said. Her voice was calm. Controlled. "We have peeled away the names. We have seen through the lies. It is time you saw them too."

Ezren's throat ached. "You don't... know what you're—"

She pressed her thumb to his forehead.

A rune flared beneath his skin.

And the cell vanished.

He was in a study.

Not a memory. A *life*.

Books stacked on every surface. A window cracked open to let in the scent of night rain and lilacs.

A fire crackled softly in the hearth.

Kaela stood at the far wall.

Not *this* Kaela. Younger. Unscarred. Her hair pulled back in a braid, her fingers ink-stained and restless.

Fire Between Us

She smiled at him.

And it *hurt*.

Because he remembered now.

This was the beginning.

Not the first *time*—but the first *betrayal*.

She crossed the room, holding a tome. "I finished decoding the sigil we found in the Ember Citadel," she said, excitement bright in her eyes. "It's a soul-binding language. Older than the ley dialects. We could use it to preserve identity through rebirth."

Ezren stood behind his desk, hands curled around the edge.

He remembered what he'd said next.

The lie.

"That's dangerous," he had told her. "It fragments the mind. Unstable."

She laughed. "Everything we do is unstable. That's the point."

He stepped around the desk. Took her hand.

"You trust me, don't you?" he asked her.

"Always."

It wasn't true.

She *hadn't*.

Not fully.

But she *wanted* to.

And he'd taken that.

Twisted it.

He remembered what happened next.

After she left—after she kissed him goodnight and vanished into the corridor, humming a lullaby from the monastery where they'd met—

He had gone to the vault.

Alone.

And rewritten the spell.

Her spell.

He had altered it at its root.

Changed the runic anchors.

Bound it not just to rebirth, but to *obedience*.

She would remember him.

Only when *he* chose.

Only what *he* allowed.

He told himself it was protection.

That the spell was too powerful for her.

That she'd been reckless.

That he was *saving* her.

He'd burned her name into the Binding and left his own deeper, hiding the truth in layers only *he* could unspool.

He thought he was keeping her safe.

Instead, he had unmade her.

And made himself a god.

Ezren screamed as the memory tore from him.

He convulsed in the cell, blood running from his nose, his eyes wide with agony.

The priest stood over him.

"Now you see," she said.

Ezren's voice was raw. "I… I loved her."

"You owned her," the priest said. "And love is not ownership."

He curled into himself, trembling.

The woman knelt again.

"There is one way forward," she said.

He looked at her.

"You must sever it," she said. "All of it. The magic, the bond, the memory. You must give her back what you stole. Even if it ends you."

Ezren closed his eyes.

And remembered her laughter.

The real one.

From that first life.

Before the Binding.

Before the loop.

Before *him.*

He saw her holding a scroll in the sun, her lips moving silently, her fingers dancing in the air as she worked out a spell not yet cast.

She had been brilliant.

She had been *free.*

He had stolen that.

And she had never known.

Until now.

They came again at dusk.

Three of them. Robes white this time. Carved with sigils of absolution.

They entered the cell without words.

Untied him.

He collapsed to the floor.

The priestess knelt again, holding a chalice of silver and shadow.

"This is your choice," she said. "Drink—and your soul will return the spell. The true Binding will be undone. She will have her magic back. Her mind. Her *self.*"

He looked up at her.

"And I?"

"You will forget."

Ezren swallowed hard.

She placed the chalice in his hands.

The liquid shimmered—violet and black, like liquified memory.

He thought of Kaela.

The look in her eyes when she stepped into the fold.

The whisper of her voice when she said, *Remember me.*

He raised the chalice to his lips.

But stopped.

"No," he said.

The priest stiffened. "What?"

He met her eyes. "I won't let you erase me. I'll return what I stole—but not with silence. Not with forgetting. She deserves to *choose* who I am. Not have me vanish like a sin washed away."

The priest's mask tilted.

Ezren stood—shaking, bleeding, burning from within.

"I will undo the magic," he said. "But I will not erase the man."

He dropped the chalice.

It shattered.

And with it, the sigils on his arms blazed—

Unraveling.

Memory peeled from his bones like smoke.

But he *held on*—

To her name.

To his guilt.

To the *truth*.

He screamed as the fire of unmaking burned through him—

And when the smoke cleared—

He stood free.

Still Ezren.

Still broken.

Still hers.

Fire Between Us

If she'd still have him.

The world returned in fragments.

First came sensation: the cold slap of stone beneath his knees, the iron stench of his own blood, and the lingering fire of magic unraveled but not extinguished. Then came sound—a distant chime, not of bells but of breaking wards. And then, finally, light. Dim and flickering.

Ezren opened his eyes.

The chamber was in ruins.

The chalice lay in molten pieces around him, its contents evaporated into smoke that clung to the walls like ghosts. The silence was thick, sacred, almost reverent—as if even the Order feared what had just happened.

He had refused absolution.

Refused erasure.

And in doing so, something ancient had *shifted*.

Not broken.

But turned.

He could feel it deep in the world's bones.

The Binding was no longer holding fast.

But neither was it gone.

It had begun to rewrite itself.

Without him.

He forced himself upright, staggering to his feet, limbs trembling with aftershocks of pain and memory. The chains had crumbled. The runes etched into his skin had faded into ash. The magic tethered to his blood—twisted, corrupted, beautiful—now pulsed quietly, free of the stolen binds he'd once hidden inside it.

His spell was broken.

But he was still whole.

Ezren looked to the corridor where the priestess had vanished.

No guards.

No footsteps.

No chase.

Just empty halls, and the echo of choices made.

He didn't waste time.

He took the first step—and nearly collapsed. His legs shook with the weight of everything he'd remembered. But he pushed forward, dragging his body down corridors etched with the memories of the thousands they had silenced, their names scratched like tally marks into the very walls.

He passed empty cells.

He passed libraries where the pages had been scoured clean by spellfire.

He passed a vault door, cracked open and weeping with whispers, where someone's identity had once been stored like a weapon.

And then, finally, he emerged into air.

Real air.

Night wind hit his face like a rebirth.

Ezren fell to his knees at the edge of the cliffside monastery, gasping for breath, watching the moon hang low and heavy over the plains.

He was out.

But not free.

Not yet.

The sky whispered with a strange song—unfamiliar, fragmented, like a lullaby sung backward. The stars themselves shimmered oddly, as though uncertain of their own positions.

Magic was rippling across the leylines, alive with the tremors of a world rewriting its own narrative.

And somewhere in that shifting tide...

Kaela waited.

He reached into the pouch stitched into the seam of his tunic. The one the Order had missed. Inside was a single shard of memory crystal, taken from the last place they had slept side by side.

He crushed it between his palms.

Blood and light spilled into the air.

And the echo of her voice whispered across the wind.

> If you're reading this... if you're listening—then it means you still remember. And that means you're still dangerous. But maybe—just maybe—you're still mine, too.

His eyes stung.

He stood.

And walked.

The hills that separated the Order's lands from the Broken Spine were jagged with magic fractures. Spells gone wild had left the landscape splintered—trees turned to stone mid-bloom, rivers suspended in mid-air, mountains curled like scrolls in the hands of angry gods.

Ezren crossed them like a penitent.

Each step hurt.

Each breath cost him.

But he didn't stop.

He couldn't.

Because with every mile, the truth inside him burned

brighter.

He *had* rewritten Kaela.

Not once.

Not twice.

Dozens of times.

To protect her.

To punish her.

To *keep* her.

He had shaped her memories like clay, convincing himself it was mercy. That it was love.

But love didn't rewrite.

Love remembered.

And Kaela—

Kaela deserved her *own* memories.

Even if those memories told her to hate him.

It took two days.

Two days without sleep.

Two days of walking through arcane storms and memory echoes that tried to drag him back into the past.

But finally—

He reached the lake.

The one carved into the Fold's edge.

The lake Kaela always returned to when she needed stillness. It hadn't been in their maps. Not in this life. Not in any clear memory.

But it was *theirs.*

And she was there.

Sitting on the dock, barefoot, her cloak tossed beside her. The reflection of stars rippled across the lake's dark surface, warping as she dragged her fingers through the water.

Ezren stepped onto the wood.

She didn't turn.

"You're late," she said softly.

His heart thudded.

"You knew I'd come."

"I always do," she said. "The question is… which you am I getting this time?"

Ezren said nothing.

He walked to her side.

Knelt.

Offered her the truth.

"I broke you," he said.

She closed her eyes.

"I rewrote your spells. Your memories. I stole your will in the name of love. And every life you've lived since… was filtered through a lie I built."

She turned her face to him.

Not angry.

Not weeping.

Just *still*.

"And now?" she asked.

Ezren exhaled. "Now I give it back."

He placed his hand against her temple.

Not with force.

Not with magic.

Just presence.

And he *opened*.

Not a spell.

Not a command.

A *surrender*.

Kaela gasped as the flood came—not just memory, but *truth*. Layer upon layer. Every loop. Every touch. Every betrayal.

The way he held her in life twenty-one.

The way he let her die in life sixty-seven.

The way he kissed her *after* he had already cast the Binding behind her back.

And the first life.

The one where they began.

Her hands clenched on the dock.

But she didn't pull away.

Not this time.

When it ended, she looked at him with a storm in her eyes.

"You took everything from me."

Ezren nodded. "Yes."

"And yet… I still love you."

Ezren swallowed.

Kaela stood.

Stepped back.

"But I don't trust you," she said.

"I know."

"And I don't know if I ever will."

"I know."

"But if we're going to end this," she said, voice iron now, "we end it *together*. With nothing hidden. No more rewriting. No more fire between us."

Ezren stood beside her.

And took her hand.

Not as magic.

Not as anchor.

Not as fate.

As choice.

And the fire between them—

Burned clean.

Fifteen

The Truth of Us

K aela rode through the northern gorge like a woman on fire.

The wind screamed past her ears, carrying the scent of storm-soaked earth and lightning-charred pine. Her horse—a pale mare borrowed from a border scout too frightened to say no—thundered over the ridgeline, hooves sparking against shards of obsidian stone.

The world around her was unraveling.

She could feel it in the way the sky cracked without thunder. In the way rivers ran backward for seconds at a time. In how birds flew in erratic spirals before dropping lifeless from the sky, wings frozen mid-beat.

Leylines frayed beneath her boots.

Time had lost its edge.

And magic was *sick*.

Still, she didn't stop.

Not even as the tremors rippled through the ground. Not even when the glow of the Fold's scar flared on the horizon like a wound pulsing open again. Not even when the memories she'd reclaimed in the Archive began to flicker and *ache* in her skull.

Not even when Ezren's voice echoed in her head—not from the present, but from every life they'd lived.

"Kaela."

"Stay."

"Choose me."

She had.

Over and over.

And he had made sure of it.

She remembered now—*all* of it. How he had taken her choices in that first life and hidden them under the guise of protection. How he had rewritten her spells, her words, her *self*.

And now he stood beside her again, whispering that it had all been for love.

Kaela gritted her teeth, fury and heartbreak surging like twin serpents beneath her ribs.

She crested the last ridge.

And saw the Fold.

Once, it had been a tear no wider than a breath. A ripple in the air, like heat on stone.

Now, it was a chasm.

A canyon of light and unmaking that split the world in two.

Reality buckled around it—trees turning inside out, mountains pulsing like lungs, colors bleeding from sky to ground and back again. The grass near the Fold shimmered in and out of seasons, blooming and dying within seconds.

The Truth of Us

Time was *leaking.*

She dismounted, stumbling forward.

The magic here burned. Not like fire.

Like *truth.*

The kind that leaves no skin unpeeled.

She dropped to her knees, the air thick with memory, her lungs struggling to pull in anything that wasn't filled with the taste of *him.*

Ezren.

Their magic still laced.

Still joined.

Still *bound.*

She slammed a fist into the dirt. "Damn you, Ezren."

But her voice shook.

Because she wasn't just cursing him.

She was cursing herself.

For how much of her heart still *wanted* to believe the parts of him that *hadn't lied.* The smile. The stillness. The nights he had watched her sleep like it hurt to blink. The way he never flinched when she broke down, when the nightmares clawed through her magic, when the spells went wrong.

He had been the only one who stayed.

Because he *made* himself stay.

Her magic crackled beneath her skin—wild, unstable. She wasn't whole. Not anymore.

And neither was the world.

Kaela forced herself to her feet, staggering toward the edge of the Fold. It pulsed like a heartbeat—too fast. Like a creature dying.

Or birthing.

She reached into her satchel, fingers trembling, and pulled

out the scroll she'd retrieved from the Archive.

The Folded Tongue.

The original spell.

Now complete.

And waiting.

Her hand hovered over it.

She could end it.

Here.

Now.

But as her magic reached for the incantation, it recoiled.

The scroll turned to ash in her hand.

Kaela stumbled back.

"What—no—"

A rune flared in the air beside her.

Not hers.

His.

The *second half* of the spell.

She had the key.

But not the door.

It had been built that way.

Because even in its inception, the Binding had required *two*. Not just for power.

For *balance*.

Her breath hitched.

Ezren.

The magic had been built on both of them. Their names. Their blood. Their *union*.

Without both—

The spell would never end.

And the world would keep breaking.

The lake was still when she found him.

Ezren sat on the old dock, legs folded, his boots beside him, feet bare in the freezing water. He didn't turn when she approached.

She stopped ten feet away, her voice a whisper torn from the wreckage of her pride.

"You knew."

He nodded.

"You built it so we'd *have* to be together."

"I built it so we'd survive," he said. "I didn't know what that would look like after."

Kaela's fists clenched. "You made me love you."

He finally turned then.

His face was raw. Sleepless. Haunted.

"No," he said. "I made you *remember* loving me. There's a difference."

She flinched.

Silence stretched between them, long and sharp.

She looked out at the lake, its surface too still, the stars in its reflection unmoving.

"I should hate you."

"You do," he said quietly. "I would, too."

Kaela's voice cracked. "But I can't fix the spell without you."

He looked at her, eyes bright with something fragile. "I know."

She knelt beside him, shoulders shaking. "I want to be free of you."

"I want you to be free."

"Then why does this still feel like love?"

Ezren reached out, slowly—no magic. No commands.

Just fingers.

He touched her hand.

The magic between them flared—not with fire.

But with memory.

Not stolen.

Shared.

Kaela closed her eyes.

And for the first time, she saw it clearly.

Not just the pain.

Not just the betrayal.

But the *truth*.

That they had built something together—flawed, cracked, but *real*. That love, once taken, had grown into something else. Something neither of them fully understood.

And it was *that* truth—

Not the spell—

That the Fold had been waiting for.

Their hands laced.

The rune between them ignited.

The Fold in the distance shuddered—

And *began to close*.

Not because of magic.

But because of *choice*.

Because even broken things can be mended.

If both sides are willing to bleed.

Kaela leaned her forehead against his.

And whispered:

"This time… we end it together."

The wind shifted.

It rolled off the lake in a low, humming current, stirring Kaela's cloak and Ezren's hair. Where their hands touched, heat pooled—not from spellwork, but from something older, deeper. A resonance that had existed beneath every vow and betrayal, beneath every rebirth and fracture.

The world recognized their choice.

And so did the Fold.

Its light on the distant horizon faltered, like a dying flame gasping in the dark. For the first time since its emergence, the rippling edges of reality stilled. Kaela felt it in her blood—the tension slackening. The crack in time wincing shut, hesitant but hopeful.

Ezren exhaled a breath that came from the bottom of his soul.

"I thought we'd lost this moment," he said softly. "That there wouldn't be a time when you would choose to stay."

Kaela didn't answer at first. She watched their joined hands, watched how her magic no longer flinched away from his touch. It curled around his in lazy spirals—no longer defensive, no longer wary.

She lifted her eyes.

"I didn't come back for you," she said.

Ezren stilled.

"I came back for the world," she continued. "For the people who never asked to bleed because we were too afraid to face the consequences of what we made."

She turned toward the Fold, her jaw tight.

"But somewhere between the pain and the spellwork, I remembered something I'd forgotten."

Ezren's voice was low. "What?"

"That we were never meant to last forever," she said. "We were meant to burn bright enough to *change something*. And we did. But the fire has to end now."

Ezren's breath hitched.

The Spells We Wove with Forgotten Words

Kaela reached into the satchel on her back and pulled out the second scroll—the *mirror* to the Folded Tongue. Inked in the old soul-language. A spell not of binding, but of *release*.

Ezren's eyes widened. "That wasn't in the Archive."

"No," Kaela said. "It was in me. Buried beneath everything you took, and everything I gave. My soul remembered what my mind couldn't."

She placed the scroll between them.

"The spell ends now. No more loops. No more forgotten lives. No more second chances."

He looked at her.

And nodded.

His hands trembled slightly as he reached into the inside of his coat and withdrew a sliver of obsidian—a memory blade, etched with runes only visible under eclipse-light. He held it over the scroll.

Kaela placed her palm atop his.

Their blood would be the final ink.

"Ready?" she asked.

"No," he said. "But I trust you."

Together, they sliced their palms.

Blood welled, then spilled, droplets falling in tandem onto the parchment. The scroll flared instantly, runes igniting with a brilliance that stung the air. The soul-language spoke itself aloud—*not from them,* but *through* them.

"By name and blood, by flame and fold, we unmake the knot we once tied."

"We remember."

"We forgive."

"We let go."

The lake erupted.

But it wasn't water that leapt.

It was *memory*.

It rose like mist—dozens, hundreds, *thousands* of Kaelas and Ezrens flickering into being. Laughing. Crying. Dying. Screaming. Kissing. Betraying. Forgiving. Their lives spiraled into the sky like shattered constellations set free.

The Fold on the horizon cracked.

Collapsed inward.

And vanished.

The sky bled white, then blue.

Time reknit itself, careful and cautious.

Kaela collapsed to her knees, gasping.

Ezren fell beside her, his hand still in hers.

And for a moment, everything was *still*.

The wind carried away the last echoes of the spell.

No one else in the world felt it.

But the earth breathed easier.

And Kaela… wept.

She wasn't sure if it was grief, or release.

Or both.

Ezren leaned against her, his voice barely audible.

"Is this what it feels like… to finally stop fighting?"

Kaela closed her eyes.

"Yes."

Their magic was still connected—but it no longer bound.

It *danced*.

Independent. Whole.

She didn't know what came next.

Didn't know if love would survive outside the spell that had shaped them.

But she knew one thing:

This time, whatever came next would be *real*.

Kaela pulled her hand free, stood slowly, and offered her palm to Ezren.

He took it.

Not because of magic.

Not because of fate.

But because she asked.

And because, despite everything, they still *chose each other*.

Sixteen

When Love Was Magic

The world bloomed in fire.

Ashes spiraled down from the broken heavens, catching in her hair like snow, glowing faintly where they touched her skin. Kaela stood atop the blackened ruins of the Skyhold, the once-gleaming fortress of her people, now a graveyard of collapsed towers and shattered sigils.

Everything was gone.

Her armor was scorched, her sword heavy with blood, her breath a cloud of pain and soot. And still, she stood. Still, she fought the ache in her bones, the grief in her throat.

And then—his shadow moved through the smoke.

She knew it before he stepped into view.

Ezren.

Not the Ezren of her waking life. This one was younger—wilder. His armor dark and streaked with firelight, his hair longer, pulled back with a strip of crimson cloth, his eyes...

gods, those eyes. They were the only thing that hadn't changed across a hundred lifetimes. Blue-gray like a coming storm, edged with something that always threatened to ruin her.

This was the first.

Their beginning.

And though she was dreaming, though the spell that held this memory was a conjuration spun from magic and longing, it felt *real*. Every heartbeat. Every breath. Every glance.

Kaela raised her blade without thinking.

Ezren stopped ten paces away, his hands empty, no weapon drawn. The air between them sparked, the remains of clashing wards and sundered oaths still humming like dying bees.

"Here to finish it?" she asked, voice hoarse.

"No," he said.

He sounded exhausted. Not with defeat. But with *choice*.

She narrowed her eyes. "You should be dead."

"I should," he agreed. "But I chose not to be."

"Cowardice?"

"Hope."

Kaela wanted to spit.

Instead, she lowered her sword an inch. "You came through the back lines."

"I didn't kill anyone on the way."

"Liar."

"I swear it."

Kaela's hands shook. Not with fear. With *knowing*. This was the moment the spell had always hidden from her—the true origin. The first *turn*.

"Why?" she demanded. "Why come here? After what you've done?"

Ezren stepped forward.

The magic between them flared, reacting to memory, to intent. The stones at their feet glowed faintly, old leyline blood remembering the shape of their confrontation.

"I came because it's over," he said. "Because I've destroyed everything. And because I couldn't bear the thought of dying without seeing your face again."

Kaela laughed, bitter and raw. "You think love can be carved from the wreckage?"

"I think love is *why* we fought," he said. "Even when we didn't know it."

She wanted to cut him down.

Wanted to sink her blade into the liar who had betrayed her people, who had cast the spell that brought her city to its knees. But her heart—damn it, her *heart*—remembered the nights before the war.

The debates.

The dances.

The secret letters folded into spellbooks.

The dreams whispered through the Veil when they didn't even know the other's name.

The connection that defied banners and bloodlines.

"You made me burn my sigil," she whispered.

"I did," he said. "And I carved yours into my spine in return."

Kaela faltered.

"I'm not asking you to forgive me," Ezren said, voice quieter now. "I'm asking you to remember."

The wind shifted.

Magic swirled between them—gold and smoke and something like starlight.

And the dream deepened.

Suddenly—

The Skyhold was whole again.

Clean, gleaming, proud.

Kaela stood on the balcony of the High Tower, dressed in the ceremonial robes of her house, her fingers wrapped around a silver goblet.

Ezren stood across from her in diplomat's black.

A truce-meeting.

But not really.

This had been their first *true* conversation.

Kaela watched her younger self move with cautious poise, her lips curving into the barest smile. Ezren's younger self was already leaning too close, already trying too hard not to look like he *needed* her approval.

"Do you always smile like you know something I don't?" she asked him.

"Only when I do," he replied.

Kaela watched them with an ache in her chest. The dream had pulled her in completely. She wasn't just remembering—she was *feeling*.

The way her pulse had quickened.

The way his voice had hooked behind her ribs and *stayed*.

"You came here with a sword," the younger Kaela whispered. "Even in peace, you wear your blade."

Ezren shrugged. "I never take it off. It reminds me not to lie."

She frowned. "That doesn't make sense."

He met her gaze.

And said, "Does anything about *us* make sense?"

The scene shifted again—another flicker—

And they were on the battlefield.

The real one.

Skyhold in flames behind them.
Her soldiers retreating.
His dying.
Kaela dropped her sword in the mud and screamed into the storm.
Ezren crawled to her, bleeding, clutching his side.
And in that moment, the past revealed its *truth*.
The memory not of their betrayal.
But of their *vow*.
Ezren reached for her hand.
And she took it.
Even surrounded by ruin.
Even shaking with rage.
Even certain that what they had could never last.
He looked up at her, eyes filled with awe and terror and love.
"You said it first," he whispered.
Kaela fell to her knees beside him, fingers locking with his.
"I did," she whispered back.
Then she closed her eyes—
And *spoke the words*.
The ones the spell had hidden from her for centuries.
The *true vow*.

> *"Even if you steal the stars from my sky, I will follow the shadow of your heart."*

The wind died.
The fire halted.
And the dream cradled her.
Because this was the moment she had forgotten.
Not their kiss.

Not their first night.
Not the betrayal.
But the *choice*.
She had *chosen* him.
Freely.
Fiercely.
Because something in her had always known that magic was not just cast from wands or words—but from *will*.
From *want*.
From *love*.
And that was when the spell shattered.
Kaela woke gasping in the campfire's ash, stars spinning above her like dizzy fireflies. Her hands trembled. Her skin burned with the residue of dream-magic.
But her heart—her *heart*—
Was whole.
And somewhere in the dark woods beyond the firelight, she heard footsteps.
Ezren.
Real this time.
No spell.
No dream.
Just him.
She stood, facing the trees, every nerve alive.
Because now, she remembered everything.
Now, she knew the truth.
And now—whatever came next—
Would be built on *choice*.

The footsteps slowed as they approached, measured and cautious, crunching faintly against the charred grass. The fire had long since died, but the embers pulsed like a second heartbeat in Kaela's ears. Her fingers hovered just above her blade, not in defense, but instinct—an echo of the battlefield that still clung to her skin like soot.

Then—

Ezren stepped into the light.

His cloak was torn, his face smeared with dirt and blood, his shirt unfastened at the collar where a rune burned faintly over his heart—one of hers. One she hadn't cast in *this* life.

A vow-mark.

Old.

Binding.

Undone.

Yet still lingering, like a ghost that refused to leave.

His eyes met hers, and Kaela saw something in them that hadn't been there before.

Not fear.

Not longing.

Not guilt.

Recognition.

"You saw it," he said quietly.

Kaela didn't answer right away.

The dream still danced behind her eyes: the ruin of Skyhold, the wine-slick balcony, the battlefield mud, and the blood that had mingled between their hands when they'd said their first impossible words.

Even if you steal the stars from my sky...

"I didn't just see it," she whispered. "I *felt* it."

Ezren took a step closer. "Then you know it wasn't all manipulation. It wasn't all lies."

She nodded, slow and tired. "Yes. But that doesn't absolve

you."

"I'm not asking to be absolved," he said.

Kaela searched his face, every line, every scar, every trace of him that had crossed a hundred versions of their story to reach her *here*. And for the first time, she understood something brutal:

He hadn't been trying to control her.

Not entirely.

He had been trying to *preserve* something that had already died.

The vow. The magic. Her *yes*.

She crossed the ashes between them. "You didn't let me grieve."

Ezren's throat worked. "I was afraid grief would make you walk away."

"I might've," she said. "But I would've done it *honestly*."

She reached up—slowly—and pressed her palm to the rune over his heart.

It flickered.

Dimmed.

And finally, went out.

Ezren flinched, but didn't pull away.

The bond was *broken*.

For real.

No more residual spells. No more loops. No more unconscious compulsions masked as love.

They were untethered.

Ezren looked down at her hand. "You're free."

Kaela's voice was steady. "And so are you."

They stood there for a long time in the hush of the night, with only wind and memory between them.

Ezren reached for her—but stopped short.

"Do you still love me?" he asked.

Kaela didn't answer.

Not immediately.

She turned her face toward the stars. They shimmered clean now. Not stolen. Not rewritten. Just sky.

"When we made the first vow," she said slowly, "we were both broken things pretending to be whole. I was a blade too eager to be used. You were a hand too desperate to hold."

He said nothing.

"I loved you then," she continued. "And again. And again. And again. But I don't want to *fall* into love with you anymore."

Ezren blinked. "What do you mean?"

Kaela met his gaze.

"I want to *choose* it."

The night exhaled.

Ezren's eyes burned.

She stepped back.

Not away.

But just far enough to create the space between them that had never existed before.

The space for *truth.*

"I don't know what that love looks like," Kaela said. "I don't know if it's softer or harder. I don't know if it's meant to last more than this lifetime. But if you want it…"

Ezren stepped forward again, into that space, slow as prayer.

"I do," he said. "This time, I do."

Kaela let him touch her fingers.

It was such a small thing.

But it shook the magic still watching from the seams of the world.

The air shimmered.
Not with prophecy.
Not with doom.
But with *possibility*.
And in that hush, in that quiet, spellless, *human* moment…
Kaela leaned into him.
And kissed him.
No fire.
No vows.
Just lips.
Just breath.
Just *them.*

And for the first time since the spell began, since the Binding first whispered their names into the seams of the stars, their love was not magic.

It was a *miracle.*
Hard-won.
Imperfect.
And *real.*

Seventeen

The Final Weaving

The moon hung low and full above the Vale of Threads, casting its pale sheen across the grasslands that shimmered with residual magic. The leyline beneath Kaela's boots pulsed like a sleeping dragon, old and coiled, waiting for the final call. Wind carried the scent of lilac and smoke, flowers blooming too early—time's laws thinning once more.

At the center of the Vale stood the Weaving Circle.

Twelve stones formed its outer ring, carved with runes so old they predated kingdoms. A thirteenth stone—fractured, scorched, and bleeding magic—stood in the center. That was where the last ritual had failed. That was where the Binding had first slipped loose. That was where time had begun to break.

Kaela stood before it, her cloak flaring in the wind, her hands bare and calloused from war, memory, and grief.

The Spells We Wove with Forgotten Words

And Ezren was beside her.

No armor. No enchantments. Just his breath in the cold, his sleeves rolled, the skin of his forearms lined with old scars and a fresh rune—*hers.*

It had been his choice.

Not bound by spell.

Not written in the old tongue.

But burned into skin as proof that he was ready to match her step for step.

No more rewriting.

No more control.

Only trust.

Kaela glanced sideways at him.

"You're sure?"

Ezren's voice was rough. "Not in the slightest."

"Good," she said. "This spell is built on uncertainty. On faith."

They stepped into the circle together.

The runes lit at once—low and red, then climbing into white-gold. Wind rose in spirals, lifting leaves from the earth, twisting Kaela's hair into a dark halo, whispering through the broken threads of magic across the realm.

"The Weaving Ritual requires dual intent," Kaela murmured, her voice steady as she raised her hands. "Not dominance. Not obedience. A *joining.*"

Ezren echoed her movements, hands mirroring hers, but a heartbeat slower. The magic obeyed them both, stretching between their fingers in threads of color—some blue, some silver, some so dark they looked like night given shape.

"Your name," Kaela said, "as it was before the first vow."

Ezren hesitated.

The Final Weaving

Then: "Ezren of the Hollow Flame."

She met his eyes. "No titles. No house."

He hesitated again.

And then, softly: "Ezren Valen."

Kaela's breath caught.

She nodded.

"My name," she said, "is Kaela Dorne."

The circle flared in recognition.

The first anchor locked.

Wind roared outward.

Above them, the stars blinked and shifted, reshaping to the old constellations—those forgotten by calendars and time, remembered only in song.

"The next step," Kaela said, "is the breath."

They turned to face each other, hands still outstretched, fingers splayed.

"You speak my truths," she whispered, "and I'll speak yours."

Ezren nodded.

Kaela took a deep breath—and spoke:

"You were the one who cast the first change. You were the one who made me forget."

Ezren didn't flinch. He responded in turn:

"You let me live, even when you should have ended me. You chose love, even when I didn't deserve it."

A pulse of magic rippled outward.

More threads rose from the ground—golden, glistening.

"You shaped my memory," Kaela said. "But I shaped your soul."

"You saved the world," he said. "But you also *saved me*."

The wind screamed.

Magic snapped like lightning between the stones, carving

new runes into the grass, etching them into the air.

Kaela stepped forward.

Ezren did too.

The space between them compressed.

Now, their hands were almost touching.

"The Weaving requires sacrifice," Kaela said, her voice quieter now.

Ezren nodded. "Name it."

She swallowed hard. "We give up the safety of forgetting."

He looked at her, gaze steady. "Then we remember."

Kaela reached out.

So did he.

Their fingers touched.

And the world *fractured.*

Not in destruction.

In *return.*

A blast of light erupted from the circle, engulfing them both, rising high into the sky like a column of fire and stars. Threads snapped across the Vale, shooting through the leylines, racing across the world like lightning across dry grass.

And everywhere—*everywhere*—people began to remember.

An old woman in a crumbling temple gasped as her husband's name returned to her tongue.

A child wept as the shape of his brother's face filled his mind.

A captain paused on the battlefield, sword lowering as the memory of why he fought crashed into him.

The Binding had stolen memory.

The Fold had broken it.

But the *Weaving* returned it.

Not neat.

Not painless.

The Final Weaving

But *true*.

Kaela's body trembled.

Ezren clutched her hand as the ritual surged to its final crescendo. They were being *seen*—not by people, but by the land itself. The stones, the rivers, the sky—all of it bore witness.

Their magic laced and merged—not consuming, but blending.

They weren't one.

They were two.

Two truths.

Two halves.

Two *wills*.

And when the light finally dimmed, when the stones stopped glowing, when the wind fell into silence again—

Kaela fell into Ezren's arms.

Not broken.

Not drained.

Whole.

They both were.

She looked up at him.

Breathless.

Burned through.

Ezren's voice was a whisper. "It worked."

Kaela nodded.

Then—quietly—she pulled a single thread of magic from her palm, glowing soft gold.

"Take it," she said.

Ezren frowned. "What is it?"

"My part of the Weaving," she said. "Keep it. Or burn it. I won't force you."

Ezren looked at the thread. At her.

And then tied it around his wrist.
The glow sank into his skin.
His voice was thick. "Then we begin again."
Not a spell.
Not a loop.
A life.
Of their own making.

The wind settled to a hush, the air still pulsing with the soft aftershock of magic reborn. Around them, the Vale of Threads shimmered—runebloom flowers blooming in arcs where ash had choked the soil hours ago, ley-grass standing straight and vibrant again. But the silence was not empty.

It was *listening*.

Kaela stood, her hand still clasped in Ezren's, her breath shaky but calm.

The Weaving had not only restored memory—it had opened the seams of the world. For the first time in centuries, the land and its people remembered themselves without filter, without edit, without enchantment.

Even the magic itself *remembered*.

She felt it now—how the world knew her. Not as a heroine. Not as a martyr. Not even as a victim of Ezren's rewriting. But as a thread in its own tapestry. One that had always burned brighter than the ones around it, even when tangled, even when frayed.

Ezren turned slowly, his expression unreadable as he took in the changed landscape.

"What happens now?" he asked.

Kaela's gaze lingered on the horizon. "Now the world remembers what it lost."

Ezren flexed his fingers. "And us?"

Kaela let go of his hand gently. "We decide what we become, Ezren. Not what we were."

He nodded. "Together?"

Kaela hesitated.

Then said, softly, "That depends."

Ezren's brow furrowed. "On what?"

She reached into her coat pocket and pulled out a fragment of crystal—dull gray, not enchanted, but smooth as riverglass. She held it out.

Ezren stared.

"A memory shard?" he asked.

Kaela shook her head. "*The* memory shard."

He went still.

"You kept it?" His voice was low, fragile.

Kaela nodded. "The night you asked me to forget you. In one of our first lives."

She placed it in his palm.

"It never broke. I think... part of me always knew I'd want to remember everything, one day. The good, the monstrous, the magic, the *truth*."

Ezren closed his hand over it.

His shoulders shook.

"You don't hate me?" he asked.

"I did," she answered without flinching. "Many times. In many lives. But hate was always too heavy for the truth to carry. And the truth is... I loved you before I ever trusted you."

She stepped forward, standing inches away.

"But I'm not the same girl you bound to your heart with a spell," she said. "And you're not the same boy who rewrote me out of fear."

Ezren nodded, his throat working as he swallowed emotion.

"So here's what we do," she said. "We write our own names—on our own pages. No spell. No vow. No loop. Just... choice."

She knelt in the grass, pulled a dagger from her boot, and pressed its flat edge to the ground. The blade gleamed, not with power, but with *clarity*. Then she drew a line in the earth.

A single arc.

Then she handed him the dagger.

Ezren knelt beside her.

And drew his own.

They touched only at the ends—barely connecting.

But together, they formed a circle.

Complete.

Equal.

Kaela whispered, "We were never meant to be a spell. We were meant to be a story."

Ezren looked at her, and for the first time, his eyes did not carry the burden of regret, or the ache of old magic.

They were simply *his*.

And they were looking only at *her*.

"So let's write it," he said.

Kaela smiled.

Not the fierce one.

Not the guarded one.

The one that had started it all—beneath firelit towers, beside scorched stone, against all logic.

She stood, wiped her hands on her thighs, and turned to face the road beyond the Vale.

The world was waiting.

Not to be saved.

But to be *remembered*.

The Final Weaving

Behind her, Ezren rose and walked at her side.
Not ahead.
Not behind.
Beside.

And as the sun broke over the stitched horizon, its rays fell across two figures walking into a world reborn—not because of prophecy, or curse, or bloodline…

But because two people, once broken by love and magic, had chosen to mend.

Together.

Eighteen

Blood for Memory

~~~~~~

The wind howled through the hollow peaks of Aelvaron, where the air itself shimmered with latent spellfire and forgotten tongues whispered from rock and sky alike. The valley stretched wide beneath a pale, bitter moon — the sky overhead boiling with cloud, yet pierced by one clear shaft of silver light that fell directly onto the stone altar at the heart of the ruins.

The Temple of the First Name.

A place older than oaths. Older than magic itself. Here, the world was young still — raw and trembling, like a wound refusing to scar.

Kaela stood at the base of the altar, her cloak whipping behind her, soaked through with rain and sweat and ash. Her fingers were cut from ritual bindings, her chest heaving, her heartbeat like thunder.

The Weaving had restored memory.

But it had not sealed it.

Across the realm, people now remembered who they were — but without a tether, those memories swelled, surged, *spilled*. Towns crumbled beneath the flood of forgotten grief. Spirits of the once-remembered wandered, half-formed and howling. The magic that had bound the realm to silence now rebelled against its own undoing.

And the ritual needed one last act.

A Keeper.

One soul.

One vessel.

To bind the words. To hold the remembering for the world — not to change it, not to distort it, but to *contain* it.

Forever.

No death. No rebirth. No release.

Just memory.

Ezren stood behind her, silent. He hadn't spoken since they arrived. His hands were clenched at his sides, his jaw tight. She could feel the tension coiled in him like a blade drawn halfway from its sheath.

Kaela stepped toward the altar.

Its surface was carved with names — not letters, but soul-script. She saw herself there. Hundreds of versions. Kaela as Queen. Kaela as traitor. Kaela as healer. Kaela as assassin. Every life she had lived. Every version Ezren had loved or broken or rebuilt.

Her throat ached.

"This is what it takes," she said.

Ezren's voice came, low and harsh. "We've done enough."

Kaela turned.

Rain dripped from her brow, ran down her cheek like tears.

"It was never enough," she said. "We undid the spell. We mended the world. But memory is a blade. It needs a sheath."

Ezren stepped forward. "Then let me do it."

Kaela shook her head. "No."

"I started this."

"So did I."

"You *rewrote* nothing."

"You still *burned* for me."

Ezren's voice cracked. "Then let me do this. Let *me* be the one who gives something back."

Kaela's eyes flashed. "You think that will fix it?"

"No," he said. "But it's mine to carry."

They stood in the shadow of the altar, the storm around them brewing harder, magic thickening in the air like the moment before lightning strikes.

Kaela clenched her fists. "If you take this, I lose you. Not just in this life. In *all* of them. The Keeper is severed from time."

"I know."

"And you'll forget me."

"No," he whispered. "But you'll forget *me*. That's the cost."

Her knees buckled. "Then we'll be strangers again. Forever."

Ezren stepped forward, cupped her face in both hands.

His touch was warm, even in the cold.

"I would rather be forgotten," he said, "than watch you fade from the world with the weight of this curse."

She shook her head, her hands over his. "I can carry it."

"You *shouldn't*."

"Neither should you."

"I *want* to."

"I *won't let you*."

Their voices rose, clashing like blades drawn beneath ancient stars.

"This isn't a punishment, Ezren!" she shouted. "It's a burden! And I *know* how to bear it—because I've lived with fragments of memory for lifetimes!"

"And I've lived with guilt," he roared. "Guilt for what I did to you. For what I *took.* Let me *give* something back!"

She pushed away from him, breath ragged.

"Don't you *dare* turn this into penance."

"It's not—"

"It *is!* And if you do this, you rob me of my choice all over again."

Ezren froze.

The wind stilled.

Only the rain fell now.

Kaela's voice broke. "Please. Don't take this from me."

Ezren looked at her, rain running down his face.

And then he smiled.

But it wasn't joy.

It was sorrow.

"I'm not taking it," he whispered. "I'm giving it."

And before she could stop him—

He turned.

Walked to the altar.

Raised his hand.

And spoke the Final Phrase.

> *"Let the world remember, and I be the cost. Let her forget, so that all others may know."*

The runes flared.

The sky split.

Kaela screamed.

"Ezren—"

Too late.

Light consumed him—violent, blinding, burning gold.

She ran to the altar, but the circle flared wide, holding her back. She slammed into it, fists against magic, screaming his name as his body lifted into the air, threads of memory pouring from his chest like stars.

His eyes met hers.

And in that final second—

She *saw* him.

All of him.

Ezren the thief.

Ezren the liar.

Ezren the boy who loved her in fire and shadow and spell.

Then—

He was gone.

In his place stood a pillar of shimmering light.

The Keeper of Forgotten Words.

The storm fell away.

The altar cooled.

And Kaela knelt in the silence, her hands on stone, tears falling without sound.

She remembered everything.

Because *he had given it to her.*

And let her go.

By choosing her, he had made her free.

By sacrificing memory, he had made her whole.

And in the wind, a whisper:

Even if you forget me, I will carry you still.

Blood for Memory

The world exhaled.
And remembered.

Kaela knelt until the world forgot how to move.

The silence that followed Ezren's final words was not hollow—it was *heavy*. It filled the Vale of Threads, echoed in the marrow of the land, resonated through time like the final toll of a sacred bell.

The sky was clear now. The storm had passed.

But the damage had already been done.

Not to the world.

To *her*.

The altar still glowed with the golden light of the Keeper's Mark, its ancient runes now infused with Ezren's essence. Kaela's fingertips trembled as she reached toward the stone, half-expecting it to burn her, to reject her. But the magic welcomed her touch with a slow, reverent warmth.

His presence lingered in the threads that clung to the altar, humming just beneath her skin like the memory of a melody once whispered in the dark.

"Ezren..." she breathed.

There was no answer.

Not with words.

Not anymore.

But the world *remembered him now*—because that was what he had chosen. Not to be her lover. Not to be her salvation. But to be a vessel for the remembering. The soul through which others could know themselves again.

Kaela stood slowly.

The light from the altar flared again—and with it came a ripple, stretching outward like a shiver across the weave of the world. She felt it move through her bones, through the stones, through the sky.

Everywhere, memories *settled*.

Not like falling ash—but like rain.

People across the realm paused as forgotten names returned to them. Daughters remembered mothers. Soldiers remembered their oaths. Poets remembered the lost verses of love songs they'd written in the shadow of war. Children remembered lullabies never sung.

The world realigned.

And yet—

Kaela's chest ached.

Because for every soul who remembered—

She was the one who had to carry the weight of what *he* had sacrificed.

He was not gone.

But he was no longer *Ezren Valen*.

Not to the world.

Not to her.

Because the Keeper could not be *loved*.

The magic forbade it.

To love the Keeper was to unravel the remembering, to return the pain of the world's loss.

It was too much for one heart.

And so the Weave had made sure to sever the thread.

He would live—forever.

He would hold the words, the memories, the names, the moments.

But he would not *feel* them.

He would not know *her*.

And Kaela—

She would remember everything.

Every moment they had stolen.

Every lie they had unspun.

Every time they chose each other.

And the one time they *didn't*.

She turned her back to the altar and began to walk.

The Vale of Threads no longer shimmered with chaos. The trees were whole. The rivers ran clear. The world had been mended.

But her heart—

Her heart remained undone.

Each step was harder than the last.

Not because of pain.

Because of *purpose*.

Ezren had given her back her freedom.

Now she had to decide what to *do* with it.

She passed through the edges of the Vale, where the great stone columns rose like broken fingers into the twilight. Each one bore a name—etched in the soul-script of those who had given something for the world's salvation.

Her name had not yet appeared.

But his—

Ezren Valen

The Keeper of Forgotten Words.

Carved in the center stone.

Kaela stopped before it, her fingers trailing across the etching.

"Do you remember me?" she asked softly.

The stone pulsed.

Then—

A breeze stirred her hair.

The Spells We Wove with Forgotten Words

And in it, faint as the hush of breath against the skin:

Even now.

Her knees gave out.
She collapsed against the monument, forehead pressed to the rune, tears falling hot and fast.
She didn't know how long she remained there.
Minutes.
Hours.
A lifetime.
Until finally, her grief dulled into clarity.
And with it, came resolve.
Kaela rose.
Straightened her shoulders.
And turned away.
She could not love him now.
But she could *honor* him.
By remembering.
By living.
By *carrying on.*
She reached into her satchel, pulled out a new spell-scroll, blank and humming with potential.
And with trembling fingers—
She began to write.
A new story.
A new vow.
Not to bind.
Not to forget.
But to remember—
And to make sure no one ever forgot *him.*

Nineteen

The Spell Unraveled

The winds screamed across the broken ridges of the Vale of Threads, carrying with them a storm of colorless ash and light. They were not winds of air, but of *magic*—fractured, screaming, alive.

Kaela stood at the eye of it all, her cloak torn and soaked, the final verse clutched in her bloodstained hands.

Around her, the world trembled.

Leylines surged and cracked like veins too swollen with power. The mountains at the edge of the horizon shimmered in and out of existence, their peaks replaced by flickers of lives that had once played out on them—soldiers kneeling in surrender, lovers clutching one another beneath starlight, a child casting her first spell.

Everywhere she turned, memory collided with reality.

And at the center of it all—

Ezren.

Or what remained of him.

He hung in the air above the altar, no longer flesh, no longer form. His essence spiraled like smoke pulled apart by storm winds—thin threads of blue fire and golden shimmer stretching upward, outward, caught between planes. The Keeper of Forgotten Words had fulfilled his purpose, and now that purpose was *devouring him.*

Kaela's voice caught in her throat as she watched another piece of him tear free—one of the last. The core thread. The tether to his name.

"No," she whispered. "Not yet."

Her fingers shook as she unrolled the scroll.

The *final verse.*

A spell written not in a single tongue, but in *all* of them. Ancient. Divine. Human. Spoken. Silent. Each line a syllable of will shaped through every version of herself that had ever lived. And only she could speak it—because only she had loved him enough to break the world to hold on.

Now she had to love him enough to *let go.*

The wind howled.

Magic screamed.

Ezren's voice—fragmented, layered in a hundred versions—rippled through the threads:

> *"Kaela... finish it."*
> *"Anchor the world."*
> *"Forget me."*

Kaela gritted her teeth, tears streaking down her cheeks as she stepped into the storm. The circle around the altar flared to life beneath her feet, the ancient runes now glowing so brightly

they scorched the stone itself.
One step.
Then another.
Every motion felt like tearing through layers of herself. Every breath scraped her lungs raw.
She reached the altar.
Her voice trembled.
Then steadied.
She began to speak the verse.

"By blood once bound and love unmade—"

A burst of wind slammed into her chest, nearly knocking her off her feet. The scroll in her hand flared, the glyphs searing into her skin as she held on.

"By name rewritten and truth relaid—"

Above her, Ezren's form writhed—each strand pulling away faster now. She saw flashes of his lives—every version of him unraveling at once. Ezren the flameborn. Ezren the rogue. Ezren the lover who stole a kingdom for her. Ezren the boy who whispered poetry into her collarbone while the world burned around them.
She wanted to fall apart.
But the verse was not yet complete.
And the world was waiting.

"Let time remember what time forgot—"
"Let love remain though form is not—"

The threads around her went still for a moment, hovering mid-air like breath suspended before the cry.

Kaela's heart stuttered.

The final line burned into her tongue.

She didn't want to say it.

She *didn't want to say it.*

Because saying it meant *ending him.*

"Let memory anchor, and shadow fade—"

She dropped to her knees, her hands to the stone, the verse completed.

"Let the Keeper's name be… unmade."

Silence.

A single, perfect silence.

The wind died.

The light folded inward.

And Ezren—

Ezren was *gone.*

The storm collapsed.

The threads fell to earth like snow.

The leyline steadied beneath her.

The altar cracked.

Kaela didn't move.

Not at first.

She sat there in the center of a healed world, surrounded by pieces of what had been Ezren Valen—pieces now dormant, still. Echoes with no voice.

The world had stabilized.

Magic was whole.

Memory was restored.

And Kaela was alone.

She rose slowly, her knees buckling. Her eyes swept the ridge and the altar, searching for *something*. A thread. A flicker. A sign.

But there was nothing.

Not a whisper.

Not a breath.

Only silence.

The kind that felt like finality.

She turned from the altar.

And walked.

For days, Kaela wandered through the lands Ezren had once saved, through forests newly green with returned names, through villages no longer haunted by ghosts of forgotten selves. People knelt as she passed, not in worship, but in *recognition*.

They knew her.

They remembered her.

Because the world had its memory again.

But Kaela—

Kaela still carried a void.

Not the kind memory could fill.

The kind *love* had left behind.

She dreamed of him. Of the way his voice had trembled when he first said her name. Of the way he always touched her like she was already fading. Of the laughter he only shared when he forgot who he was supposed to be.

In every lifetime, they had found each other.

And in this one—

They had chosen to let go.

But on the seventeenth day, in a city carved into the cliffs of the western sea, as Kaela stood atop a high balcony watching the tide pull silver across the sand, a breeze shifted.

It was subtle.

Barely there.

But it *carried a name.*

Not spoken aloud.

Not whispered.

Felt.

Kaela turned.

There, in the market square below, stood a figure wrapped in traveler's garb—hood up, cloak dark, posture weary. He moved like a man not used to his own limbs. Like someone relearning gravity.

He paused at the edge of the crowd.

Turned.

And looked up.

She couldn't see his face.

But she knew the eyes.

Ezren.

Her heart stopped.

He didn't wave.

Didn't speak.

But the tether between them—

It *tugged.*

Not the old bond.

Something new.

A thread reborn, spun not from spell or fate or prophecy—

But from *choice.*

Her knees weakened.

The Spell Unraveled

She gripped the balcony rail.
He smiled.
A small, uncertain thing.
And then—
He was gone.
Vanished into the crowd.
Kaela stood there a long time, trembling, breath catching on a storm that refused to break.
He was not the Keeper anymore.
He should have been *unmade.*
And yet—
Something had *survived.*
A sliver of soul.
A shard of will.
Or maybe…
Maybe love was never meant to vanish.
Even when the spell unraveled.
And perhaps—
Just *perhaps*—
Their story wasn't over yet.

Kaela ran.
She left the balcony, boots slamming against stone, heart thundering louder than her footsteps as she pushed past startled merchants and wide-eyed children. The air was thick with salt and magic, the sea breeze laced with something warmer—something *old.*
Something *his.*
She didn't call his name.
She couldn't.
To speak it now might shatter the spell of it all. Might draw

attention to a miracle not meant for witnesses. Might *chase him away.*

Because what she saw—what she *felt*—had no name in any language spoken or sung.

Ezren had been unmade.

Unwoven from the threads of the Keeper's binding. His soul had fractured and dispersed into the world. She had seen it. Had *felt* the spell finish, had spoken the last verse with her own mouth.

She had let him go.

And yet…

The shape she'd seen in the crowd—shoulders cloaked in shadow, that uncertain tilt of the head, the storm-gray eyes beneath the hood—it was him. Not the man she had known, but a shadow of him. A beginning.

Kaela rounded a corner, the stone corridor narrowing into an alley. Ahead, the open square spilled out onto a harbor soaked in gold from the setting sun.

Boats rocked lazily in their moorings.

Sails flapped like slow breath.

Fishermen hauled nets heavy with glimmering silver things that shimmered too brightly to be mere fish.

But he wasn't there.

Only the echo of him.

The *feeling*.

Kaela slowed, breath tearing through her throat as she scanned the crowd.

A child bumped into her, chasing a rolling hoop. An old woman offered her a charm against bad dreams. A pair of lovers leaned into each other at the fountain, lost in a whisper Kaela couldn't hear.

The Spell Unraveled

No Ezren.

No shadow.

Nothing.

Kaela stepped into the fountain square and turned in a full circle. Desperation pricked her like thorns beneath the skin.

She reached for her magic.

Not to cast.

To *sense*.

To search the threads.

They had always been able to find each other through the web of magic, across lifetimes, across time-loops, across war and peace and betrayal. It had been the one constant—his signature, warm and erratic, like flame caught in wind.

She reached deeper.

Deeper.

And there—*faint*, so faint—

A flicker.

A single strand of light, drifting at the edge of perception.

It wasn't quite his old magic. Not the fire, not the twist of time. This was something *quieter*. Gentle. Unformed. As if he had not been reborn—but *remade*.

Kaela turned toward the harbor.

The thread pulled her there, barely brushing her consciousness like the memory of a touch.

She followed it.

Down stone steps slick with sea salt.

Past gulls perched like sentinels.

Toward the smallest of the piers, where a single skiff floated untethered, bobbing in time with the tide.

A figure stood beside it.

Hood lowered now.

Hands bare.

His back to her.

She stopped.

A breath caught between centuries.

"Ezren," she said, barely a whisper.

He turned.

And *everything stopped.*

It was him.

But not quite.

His face was younger, smoother—untouched by the lifetimes of war and memory. His eyes were the same storm-gray, but behind them was *emptiness.* Not hollow.

Clean.

His brow furrowed. "Do I know you?"

Kaela's heart cracked.

He didn't *remember.*

Of course he didn't.

The Keeper's sacrifice had cost him *everything*—his past, his love, *her.*

But something else lingered. He didn't move away. Didn't recoil. His gaze lingered on her like a man seeing a painting he couldn't name but somehow *knew* he'd dreamed once.

"No," she said gently, "you don't."

He stepped forward, uncertain.

Kaela didn't speak.

She reached into her coat and pulled free a folded parchment—the final fragment of the Weaving. The one she hadn't burned.

She handed it to him.

Ezren took it, fingers brushing hers.

The moment they touched—

The Spell Unraveled

Magic surged.

A *spark*.

A golden flare that flashed between their palms and vanished just as quickly.

He inhaled sharply.

"What was that?" he asked, blinking.

Kaela's smile trembled. "A beginning."

He stared down at the parchment.

Then back at her.

"Will I see you again?"

Her throat tightened. "If you choose to."

Ezren nodded slowly. "Then I think I will."

And for the first time in days, weeks, *lives*, she let herself believe it.

That what had been unmade could be *rewoven*.

Not with spells.

Not with fate.

But with *choice*.

With time.

With *hope*.

As he stepped into the skiff, sail unfurling with a quiet whisper, Kaela stood at the end of the pier, her hands clenched at her sides.

The sun dipped lower.

And just before the boat turned from shore, Ezren looked back.

One last time.

And smiled.

Not in recognition.

But in *possibility*.

Kaela whispered to the wind, the last line of a story she never thought would end:

"Even if we forget, we will find each other."

And the sea carried it away.

Twenty

The Name in the Wind

The wind moved strangely that day.

It didn't howl or sing. It *listened.*

Kaela felt it the moment she stepped off the broken causeway leading into the town of Myrwaith—an old settlement folded against the cliffs, known more for its salt-baked stones and highbird markets than for magic. The air held that old pull she'd tried to forget: the quiet thrill that whispered across her bones when a spell, forgotten or forbidden, stirred somewhere near.

She hadn't come looking.

Not for magic.

And certainly not for *him.*

It had been years.

Since the ritual.

Since the anchor.

Since she had watched Ezren's soul fracture into the winds

of magic, his name carried off like dust in sunlight, burned clean from the world so others could remember.

She had traveled far from the Vale of Threads, built a life without altars or ancient languages. She'd traded runes for ink and taught spellweaving in the southern academies. Taught students to respect the weave, to fear what had once been beautiful and deadly and hers.

She never spoke his name.

She *never spoke his name.*

And yet—

She heard it in the wind now.

Not the name itself.

But the weight of it.

The cadence of syllables long hidden beneath the world's breath.

Kaela turned her head slightly, her gaze narrowing.

The market was as mundane as any she'd known—children darting between vendors, spices flaring sweet and sharp in the breeze, a young girl laughing as a painted bird perched on her wrist.

But somewhere, from the edge of it—

Someone was *chanting.*

Not a song.

Not a prayer.

A *spell.*

Kaela moved.

Her boots scuffed dust as she followed the sound through the maze of canvas stalls and shaded walkways. It was soft, but sure. She passed by a wind-chime stand, a woman selling charmed bells, a tall mirror that reflected not her own image, but a glimpse of herself in another life—hair darker, eyes sharper, blood on her cheek.

The wind caught it again:

"...even if the sky breaks..."

Kaela's breath stilled.

That line.

That was the fourth verse of the *Spell of Holding Between Worlds*—the one she and Ezren had forged beneath a dying eclipse, hidden from the world, rewritten a thousand times through a hundred lives.

No one alive should know that spell.

Not anymore.

Not unless—

She turned a corner.

And stopped.

A small crowd had gathered at the edge of the square. Children mostly. A few elders, crouched on worn stone steps, all watching a boy—barely sixteen—stand atop an overturned crate. His hands moved in careful, deliberate patterns.

And from his lips:

"...I will follow the thread even when cut. I will answer the name even when unspoken."

Kaela's chest tightened.

The wind surged.

The boy had soft brown hair and dust on his cheek. His voice was low, not theatrically so, but with the kind of weight one carried without understanding why. And his eyes—

Gods.

Storm-gray.
The same shade.
The same shape.
Ezren.
But not.
He didn't look at her. Didn't *see* her. His gaze was distant, eyes unfocused, like the spell itself was speaking through him.

She moved through the crowd, heart pounding. Her fingers trembled, a dozen runes sparking along her skin unbidden, reacting to the magic in the air.

The boy's voice deepened.

He was reaching the end.

"…and when the world forgets me, I will not forget myself."

He paused.
Rain began to fall—light, silver, warm.
Kaela stepped forward.
He looked at her.
For the first time.
The market hushed.
Children stilled.
Wind coiled.
Kaela stared into his face.
And saw *him.*
Ezren.
No memories.
No spell-bound weight behind his eyes.
But something…
A shimmer.

The Name in the Wind

A recognition not of thought, but soul.
The boy spoke the final line.

"…for my name lives in the wind."

The air cracked.
A soundless thunder rolled through the square.
Every chime in the wind-stand behind him rang at once.
The runes flared beneath Kaela's skin.
And she smiled.
Tears welled in her eyes, unbidden, burning.
"Found you," she whispered.
The boy blinked, confused.
But the wind answered her.
It *shifted.*
Spun.
Rushed through the crowd like an embrace.
And from its curl—
A single whisper:

Kaela.

Her knees nearly buckled.
Because it wasn't the boy who'd spoken.
It was the *wind.*
And the boy—
He tilted his head.
"I know you," he said.
Kaela's voice was cracked and broken and whole.
"Not yet," she said. "But you will."
He stepped down from the crate slowly, eyes searching hers.

"What's your name?" he asked.

She smiled through tears.

And told him.

Then asked: "What's yours?"

He hesitated.

Then, slowly, as if remembering a dream he hadn't yet dreamed, he said:

"...Ezren."

The wind shivered.

And began to *remember*.

The wind swirled between them, warm and sharp like the edge of a blade that had forgotten it once drew blood. Kaela stood rooted to the flagstones, her name still lingering in the air around her like a benediction — or a curse. The boy — *Ezren,* he had said — looked at her as if he were peering through time itself, trying to decipher the shape of a life he hadn't lived.

Yet.

Kaela's throat was thick with memory. Her fingers ached with spells unsaid. And her heart—her heart, stitched so carefully over the years—had begun to unravel again, thread by thread.

She took a breath and closed the space between them.

The boy didn't flinch. His eyes searched hers, and for a moment, Kaela saw the flicker of something old and wounded and *wondering* flash through them. He didn't understand what he had said, not truly. But the words had come to him. As if whispered on the breath of the world.

"Do you know what that was?" she asked softly, not trusting her voice to hold firm.

He shook his head, brow furrowed. "It was… a poem. Or

a dream. I've been hearing it in pieces. Since I was a child. In sleep. In wind. When I walk near rivers or under eclipsed moons. I write it down. I don't know why."

Kaela smiled through her tears. "You remember."

"Do I?" he asked.

Kaela nodded, eyes shimmering. "You will."

A pause stretched between them. Not awkward. Not uncertain. But sacred.

He glanced down at his hands, where a faint shimmer still traced the rune-gestures he'd formed in the air minutes ago. His voice dropped to a whisper. "It scared them. The spell. I didn't mean to frighten anyone."

"You didn't," Kaela said. "You reminded them."

He looked up. "Of what?"

Kaela took his hand.

Her fingers closed around his — smaller than hers now, callus-free, clean of blood and guilt — and held them gently, as one might cradle a match just before lighting it.

"Of who you were," she said. "Of who you are. And who you still might be."

The crowd had dispersed, the market forgotten. Time itself seemed to hover around them, holding its breath.

Ezren blinked at her again, confused. "I've never met you before."

Kaela's smile was full of sorrow and joy. "You did. Once. A long time ago. In a hundred lives. And I loved you in every one."

The boy's breath caught.

"But we broke the spell," Kaela continued, her voice barely above the wind. "We ended the loop. We gave the world its memory back. You chose to vanish. To become the Keeper.

You gave *everything*."

He was quiet for a long time. Then:

"Then why am I here?"

Kaela looked up at the sky. The clouds were thinning. Light was breaking through in strands, like a tapestry slowly unraveling its secrets.

"I don't know," she whispered. "Maybe the world needed you again. Maybe the spell wasn't done with us. Maybe… love writes its own endings."

The boy's hand tightened in hers. "Do you want me to remember?"

"No," she said. "Not unless you choose it."

He was silent.

Then — softly — "Could you stay?"

Kaela's heart cracked and healed in the same breath.

"I was hoping you'd ask."

They stood in the market square as the sun dipped low, the wind curling around them, not fierce, not tragic — but familiar. It whispered between rooftops, danced through chimes, tugged gently at cloaks and hair, brushing the edges of time.

Not to erase.

But to *begin*.

And somewhere, far away, in a hidden grove where old magic slumbered, the altar of the Keeper cracked open — just slightly.

And a single thread of golden light slipped free.

Carried by the wind.

Toward a future not written in runes or spells or sacrifice.

But in *choice*.

Kaela and Ezren—boy and woman, soul and shard, past and possible—turned away from the square together.

One step.

Then another.
Not to reclaim what was lost.
But to create something new.
The End.

www.ingramcontent.com/pod-product-compliance
Lightning Source LLC
LaVergne TN
LVHW011936070526
838202LV00054B/4671